The Ways of the Wind

RODNEY HOWARD-BROWNE

River Publishing

THE WAYS OF THE WIND

Copyright © 2024 by Rodney M. Howard-Browne

Unless otherwise noted, all scriptures are from the King James Version (KJV): King James Version, public domain.

Scripture quotations taken from the Amplified® Bible (AMPC), Copyright © 1954, 1958, 1962, 1964, 1965, 1987 by The Lockman Foundation. Used by permission. www.lockman.org

Published by River Publishing
P.O. Box 292888, Tampa, FL 33687 USA

ISBN: 979-8-89298-725-7

Printed in the United States of America

CONTENTS

Introduction ix

1 The Wind of God: Part One
It's Not About Comfort; It's About Change 1

2 The Wind of God: Part Two
Blown by the Wind to Do the Master's Bidding 29

3 The Necessity of the Anointing: Part One
Learning the Ways of the Wind 63

4 The Necessity of the Anointing: Part Two
It's All About Yieldedness 91

Postscript 106

About the Author 107

Connect 110

Other Books and Resources by Rodney Howard-Browne 111

The River at Tampa Bay Church 115

River University 117

River School of the Bible Online 119

God Wants to Use You to Bring in the Harvest of Souls! 120

INTRODUCTION

My friends, there is so little time left now, and the Wind of God is blowing, ready to usher in the soon-coming King. The choice is yours—do you want to be carried by the Wind? Do you want to be a carrier of the Wind of the Spirit of God? Do you want to speak and release the Wind of the Holy Ghost? Or do you want to watch the Wind blowing others?

Just as a pilot or a sailor studies the wind that blows across the Earth, so we must learn the ways of the Wind of the Spirit as He blows across the Earth. The Bible tells us that the wind blows where it listeth (John 3:8)—no man can dictate to the wind. Likewise, we cannot dictate to the Holy Ghost where He should blow or how He should blow. Rather, we must learn to go with the Wind and be blown by the Wind of God.

Following Him is our protection. He'll lead us into the right places at the right time, and He'll lead us out again. He'll breathe life into what is dead and dying, and bring restoration, healing, and deliverance. When we know the ways of the Wind of the Holy Ghost, we will be a mystery. The devil will not be able to find us or follow us. No man or obstacle will be able to stand in our way, and we will be able to be blown into cities and nations, seeing people touched, saved, healed, and changed.

INTRODUCTION

The Wind of the Holy Ghost will carry us, sustain us, provide for us, and strengthen us. And when we speak, we will carry His cry and His authority. As we yield to Him, we will be unstoppable. And this is how God wants us to live.

This is essential for these end-times, where we need to hear His direction for each day. He has great plans for each one of us and He has a great work for us to do. But we must be yielded and totally surrendered to Him. We have to let go of our flesh, pride, fear, and we must let the Wind of the Holy Ghost blow *in* us and then *through* us. We must get rid of religion and tradition and be open to do things His way. For how can He do a new thing when we are holding on to the old things?

We must take the Wind of God to a lost and dying world. We must take the mighty rushing Wind Who can blow and transform, renew, and restore.

In this book, I will show you how to flow and be carried by the Wind of the Holy Ghost, and how to recognize the Wind and stay in the Wind. I will show you blockages and hindrances to flowing in the Wind of Holy Ghost, and I will show you how learning the ways of the Wind will take you and your ministry to another level. Will you choose to follow the Wind of the Holy Ghost? Will you yield to Him? The decision is yours.

FOR THE HARVEST,

DR. RODNEY HOWARD-BROWNE

1

THE WIND OF GOD: PART ONE

It's Not About Comfort; It's About Change!

Go to John 3:8:

> The wind bloweth where it listeth, and thou hearest the sound thereof, but canst not tell whence it cometh, and whither it goeth: so is every one that is born of the Spirit.

Now look at that verse in the Amplified Version (Classic Edition):

> The wind blows (breathes) where it wills; and though you hear its sound, yet you neither know where it comes from nor where it is going. So it is with everyone who is born of the Spirit.

THE WAYS *of the* WIND

I want to talk to you about THE Wind. Not just any wind, I want to talk to you about the Wind of Almighty God. And I want to tell you that you're not reading this by chance, you're not reading this by accident, you are reading this by *divine appointment*. Whether you realize it or not, you have been blown to read this by the Wind of the Spirit of God.

And the Wind of the Lord has blown you and brought you to this place and this hour.

THE WIND OF GOD BLOWS ON YOU AND IN YOU

> *You are not those who will live the mundane. You are not those whose life will go on into oblivion, whose life will go into eternity with nothing to carry. You are those handpicked by the Master who will carry this Good News—the Gospel—with power, signs, and mighty wonders, seeing the nations of the Earth shaken.*

Now the Wind of God works a little differently than natural winds because the Wind of God not only blows *onto* someone, but blows *in* them. When the Wind of God blows in you, something happens—you are moved and you are moved to places that you know not of.

There are times when you can't even intellectualize where the Wind is blowing you, but you know that you are being blown by the Wind. And there are those who will try to work out which way you are blowing, but they cannot know because it is the Wind of the Spirit of God.

And He moves this one over here, and He moves that one over there, all for His divine purpose and His divine plan. For He sees from Heaven, and He knows exactly what needs to be accomplished for this end-time move. And I believe with all my heart that we stand on the brink of the greatest move of God this world has ever seen. I believe we're standing on the brink of the greatest harvest of souls that the Church has ever seen. I believe we're standing on that which even the prophets of old prophesied, and the Bible says that the prophets longed to see our day (Matthew 13:17). But here you are, handpicked by the Holy Ghost, handpicked by God, because God has a specific plan for your life.

You are not those who will live the mundane. You are not those whose life will go on into oblivion, whose life will go into eternity with nothing to carry. You are those handpicked by the Master, who will carry this Good News—the Gospel—with power, signs, and mighty wonders, seeing the nations of the Earth shaken.

> *The Wind of God does not only blow onto someone, but blows in them. And when the Wind of God blows in you, something happens.*

YOU CANNOT STOP THE WIND OF GOD

Remember, the enemy always wants to stop the Wind. He always tries to put it in a box. But you cannot put the Wind of God in a box. Can America stop a hurricane? Can Washington, D.C. house a hurricane? No! Well, if you cannot even stop a storm on the Earth, you certainly cannot touch the Wind of Heaven. And when the Wind of God comes and blows, He brings change.

You may have wondered about your life and ministry. You may have even questioned, "God, why would You have me go there? Why would You have me do this? But Lord, this even feels uncomfortable for me." But God says, "Just follow Me. I'm blowing you by My Spirit, because if you don't go with Me here, you can't go with Me over there. I'm bringing you through and bringing you into that place."

If you climb the high mountains of the Earth, it's great to stand on the peak and look over the view, but oh, what a journey to the top! Likewise, have you ever questioned, "God, I do not understand some things. Why do You take me here? And why do You take me there?"

Some people may look at you and think you're a little strange because you don't blow in formation, but that's because they would like to control the Wind of the Spirit of God. They say, "We don't want the mighty rushing Wind. We just want a gentle breeze! This Wind that came through and took the leaves off the tree, we don't want that. We don't want the branches to shake."

But I tell you, the Wind of God is blowing and no man can stop it. I say again, the Wind of the Spirit of God is blowing and no man can stop it! Oh, hallelujah! You signed up the day you gave your life to Jesus. Your life is not your own. You were bought with a price and you belong to Him (1 Corinthians 6:20).

YOU HAVE TO LET GO OF THE FAMILIAR
The Wind of God says, "I want you to go here," and you go here. He says, "I want you to go there," and you go there. At any time you could stop, but you say, "Lord, breathe on me," and then He comes again with great intensity. And you say, "Oh Lord, I feel that same unsettling. It's like I'm coming out of my comfort zone. Lord, everything that I've been resting on has been moved. It's being shaken." He replies, "Yes, but you said, 'Lord, take me higher. God, take me into the place that You have for me.' And in order for you to go higher, you have

to let go of that which was familiar. You have to let it go."

Perhaps you have given up houses and lands, or maybe you have given up your job to come to River University. You have paid a great price. If you have been called of God into the work of God in the ministry, you can think back to the day when you accepted the call and the great changes you made. Maybe you stepped out of the business world, laid aside your house, your car, your prestige, and your possessions. You didn't understand why you were doing it, but the Wind of God came upon you. It's because the Wind blows you where He wants you to go.

It's like pieces on a board game. We may think that some pieces are not necessary. Like the little pawn on the chessboard that's just moving one little square at a time, but one day, it is going to be a king. (If you know anything about the game of chess, you'll know that the little pawn can only move one square. It doesn't have the ability or the movement of the bishop piece. In contrast, the bishop has a lot of movement).

Maybe you don't even know who you are. You don't even realize what God has planned for you. You are looking at your life in the natural, and your life seems torn by the storms of life. But that's because another wind has been blowing at you—the wind of defeat. The wind of the lies of hell have come against you to destroy you. You've said, "Can God do something with my life? Can God do something?" And the Lord says, "Yes, don't be afraid." Because when He blows upon you, something's going to happen. It does not matter where you live. It does not matter what your education is. Again, I say that you are not reading this by accident, you are reading this by divine purpose.

THE WAYS *of the* WIND

THE WIND IS NO RESPECTER OF PERSONS

> *The Wind blows upon each and every individual, because it's the Wind of God.*

The Bible says in Acts 2:1–2b, "And when the Day of Pentecost was fully come, they were all with one accord in one place. And suddenly there came a sound from heaven as of a rushing mighty wind." I want you to know that same sound is still coming in this day and in this hour.

And something about the wind is that it is no respecter of persons. If the winds of a hurricane are blowing, they'll blow the same on the strong and the weak. And they don't stop at one house, all houses are affected by the wind. And God is no respecter of persons, it does not matter what nationality you are.

The Wind does not stop when it gets to the Chinese. The Wind does not stop at the Japanese, the Arabs, the Jews, the Greeks, or the Africans. The Wind blows upon each and every individual, because it's the Wind of God.

Someone says, "What's that I'm feeling?" It's the Wind of Heaven blowing on you. Someone says, "What's that I'm sensing on the inside of me?" It's the Wind of the Holy Spirit blowing upon you.

THE WIND DOES NOT MAKE SENSE TO YOUR NATURAL MIND

> *When the Wind of God blows you, you'll say, "I'll never do that," and then you'll do it. And then you'll say, "I don't understand that because I said that I'd never do that." But you cannot dictate the way of the Wind.*

Dr. Lester Sumrall quit everything and left house, land, church, and ministry, and moved locations seven times during the course of his ministry. Seven times he uprooted! No matter what happened, no matter what great ministry he had built, he uprooted and moved as the Wind moved.

When the Lord called him to go to the Philippines, it is such a powerful story. He landed in the Philippines and for six months absolutely nothing happened. He couldn't even get one person saved—not one person saved! He witnessed to people, handed out tracks, but nobody would listen to him.

Ministers over here in the United States did whatever they could to try to help him and sent over tracts, books, and Gospel films. Dr. Sumrall had a warehouse stashed full of all the stuff he would need to have a great evangelistic crusade. Yet, he could not even get the doorman at the hotel saved! And Dr. Sumrall was almost in a state of depression. One day, he turned the television on, and there on the news was a woman being bitten by devils in a prison cell. Viewers could see the bite marks appearing on her arms. And the Lord said to Dr. Sumrall, "Go there and cast the devil out of her." Dr. Sumrall said, "Lord, do you want me to do it?" The Lord said, "Go." So Dr. Sumrall went to the jail, and it was put on national television. There in the prison, he cast the devil out of this woman, and within the next six months, he had over 300,000 people give their lives to Jesus.

What a great revival hit Manila, Philippines. What a great move of God hit that nation. And I asked Dr. Sumrall, "Why did you leave?" He said, "I had to leave because if I had not left, they would have worshipped me."

I thought, *In the natural, it doesn't even make sense. What man would walk away from a national revival?* But he said, "I had to.

They were falling down in the streets, worshiping me." Because people in foreign countries worship certain gods and then they change and they just worship whatever they find. Dr. Sumrall knew they would form their own cult and worship him. So, he left.

Somebody says, "What happened?" The Wind blew him into the Philippines and the Wind blew him out. The Wind doesn't make sense many times to the natural mind. When the Wind of God blows you, people are not going to understand you. When the Wind of God blows you, *you're* not even going to understand yourself!

When the Wind of God blows you, you're going to find yourself doing things that you never even dreamed were possible. You're going to be pinching yourself and saying, "Truly this can't be me. I never even saw myself in this position, and I feel totally inadequate for the job."

When the Wind of God blows you, you'll say, "I'll never do that," and then you'll do it. And then you'll say, "I don't understand that because I said I'd never do that." But you cannot dictate the way of the Wind.

THE WIND KNOWS NO DISCRIMINATION

I sense in my spirit there's a stirring taking place on the inside of people reading this. There's a stirring, a deep stirring by the Spirit of God because the Lord's getting you ready. He's preparing you for that which He will have you do in this final hour. It matters not how young or how old you are. The Wind knows no discrimination. The Wind is no respecter of persons.

The eyes of the Lord run to and fro throughout the whole Earth; God is looking for men and women to whom He can show Himself strong on their behalf (2 Chronicles 16:9). All you have to do is just throw up your hands and say, "Lord, I don't feel within myself that I even have what it takes, but God, I just yield myself to You. Wherever You want to blow and wherever You want me to go, I'll go. I'll do what You want me to do, I'll say what You want me to say, and I'll be what You want me to be."

You might be reading this and saying, "I remember there was a time when I felt that Wind. I felt the Wind of Heaven blowing me and moving me, but something's happened, and I don't feel that anymore." I pray that right now there comes the stirring by the Holy Ghost on the inside of you.

People will try to put you in a box, and they'll try to make you conform, but don't allow it to happen. God says, "My Wind has placed you there. My Wind has put you there. My Wind has blown you there for a purpose to see that nation touched." So even now, a fresh wind blows, and even now, a new resolve will come. For the glory of God will sweep the nation, and the fire of God will be made manifest, and the nation shall know Almighty God.

I sense in my spirit that there's a stirring taking place on the inside of people reading this. There's a stirring, a deep stirring by the Spirit of God because the Lord's getting you ready. He's preparing you for that which He will have you do in this final hour.

WAIT ON THE WIND

If you are in River University, God has placed you here within this ministry. You've been called and handpicked by the Lord for a time of preparation. Some are called to stand and hold up the hands at R.M.I. (Revival Ministries International), and you'll be a vital part of the work. For others, when the time shall come, the Spirit of God will launch you into that which He has for you. Do not try to work it out and don't try to step out prematurely. Wait on the Wind, for the Wind will let you know.

There'll come a stirring by the Spirit of God, deep down on the inside of your heart, and you'll live with it, eat it, walk it, sleep it, drink it, and you'll breathe it. It'll come out in your dreams, and it'll come out in the night hours. But if you step out prematurely, you'll look for the Wind and you'll not find it. But wait upon the Spirit of God, and allow the Holy Ghost to place you in the divine incubator of the Spirit—where you can be prepared and trained, so that you are fully equipped. Then when you are launched, you'll go out by the Spirit of God. You'll go like an arrow, and you'll go with precision. You'll go right into the bull's-eye of the enemy, and you'll do exactly what the Holy Ghost has planned and purposed for your life. So WAIT upon the Wind. Do not be impatient. Do not say, "I think I'll do this. I think I'll do that." No! For you know not the way of the Wind. Listen carefully to the Holy Ghost and follow His promptings, because many take detours and they spend five or ten years out in the wilderness trying to find the Wind again.

> *Those who believe the Lord will not make haste but will be patient knowing that He knows exactly what He is doing.*

Some are even blown back by the Spirit of God to the place where they first felt the Wind, or where they last felt the Wind. And then their sails are filled again, and they begin to move forward, being propelled by the Unseen One into that place Heaven has for them. Don't be impatient, for He's not impatient. Those who believe the Lord will not make haste, but will be patient knowing that He knows exactly what He is doing.

THE WIND OF GOD: PART ONE

HE KNOWS WHAT HE IS DOING!

God knew exactly what He was doing when He first called us to America, and you've probably heard the story—maybe you could tell it better than I can! But I remember when we came here, things were pretty uncomfortable. We were coming to a new country, there was a culture shock of driving on the wrong side of the road, then my hand was eaten by the trunk of a Lincoln Town Car at the airport because I didn't know that when the trunk closes, it actually cranks down. I thought there was something stuck, so I put my hand in there and got it caught in the trunk of the car and screamed out loud. They popped the trunk and my hand was bleeding. It's one thing to be in Africa and be attacked by a lion; it's another thing to be in Louisville, Kentucky, and attacked by a black Lincoln Town Car. How dangerous could it get?

I came into this country with my wife and three little ones, and we didn't know exactly all of that which the Spirit of God was telling us to do. Some people thought we were crazy and said, "There goes poor old Rodney and Adonica, with nobody but God."

We stepped out because we felt an intense burning on the inside of us—something to do with America. I couldn't put it all into words, but every time I saw the American flag and heard "The Star-Spangled Banner (Francis Scott Key)" I began to weep uncontrollably. So much so that I carried a cassette tape in my car with just "The Star-Spangled Banner" on it, so I could hear it over and over again. People back in my homeland thought I was crazy and couldn't understand why I was born in South Africa, yet I lived America, talked America, ate America, prayed America, and breathed America! I even went down to the store to find some taco shells, so that I could go home and make myself a little taco because I wanted to be in America. All because I felt this Wind just blowing me.

Even when Adonica and I went out on a date and were sitting in the restaurant, looking into each other's eyes, instead of whispering sweet nothings in each other's ears, all we talked about was America, and we sang "The Star-Spangled Banner." We couldn't get away from it because we felt this propelling by the Unseen One. People said, "Well, do this and do that, and go here and go there," and I said, "I can't." They said, "You don't have all your ducks in a row. You need to answer these questions. What about this? What about that?" And I said, "I don't know about this, and that, and the other thing. I just know that I feel something's happening on the inside of me."

And then when we came over to the U.S. we said, "Now what?" And often, when people come into that same place, they quit because they don't see the breakthrough immediately. Things were tough. We couldn't get a vehicle because we couldn't get credit. I didn't even have a Social Security number. If it wasn't for the bank manager who was the friend of a friend of ours who gave us a Social Security number of 000-00-0000, we couldn't have opened a bank account, and that was a miracle in itself. After that, for two years my Social Security number was 000-00-0000.

It was unheard of and she probably could have got into trouble, but thank God I was a zero! And it was uncomfortable to come from Africa in December in the middle of our summer to the middle of winter in the U.S., with ice on the roads, everything frozen, and the blue skies disappearing for months. And when we landed in America, things were in turmoil in the Church, much as they are right now—for things have come full circle.

The Church at that time had no joy, or there were one or two rare sightings of joy. But for the most part, joy was extinct in the Church. If people wanted joy, they had to go down to the museum and look in the glass cage and say, "That was joy. It lived several thousand years ago in the early Church," and the curator of the museum stood there with a slight smile on his face and said, "Yes."

So we started having meetings and I remember preaching for a main denomination. I preached Sunday night, and there were several thousand people there. I called Adonica, and she flew in with the kids. We were all excited because this was a great breakthrough. We'd been in the country one month, and here we were in this big church, and I preached a message called, "Getting Ready for the Coming Move of God."

Right after the service, the head of the denomination came to me and said, "That was a powerful message. I'm going to give you the cassette tape of tonight. And I want to write a letter to give to you, and I'm going to give you the addresses to all of our five hundred churches. I thought, *This is it! The breakthrough has come. We've been here one month. We'll send the letter to these 500 churches. What a breakthrough.* If you came to new country and suddenly, you'd gotten into this major church, who'd given you the tape of the night, and the head overseer had given you a signed handwritten letter that would open up major doors to you all over the 500 churches, then you'd think it was a breakthrough too!

I was excited, and I grabbed the tape and the letter, and the Lord said, "No!" I said, "What? What do You mean, 'No,' God? What do You mean, 'No?' This is a good plan. This will quicken things up. This will speed things up. Lord, within twelve months we'll be booked from here to Waxahachie."

And the Lord said to me, "Go ahead; book yourself up. But son, you'll spend five years trying to find what I really have for you here." He said, "Don't do it. If you do, you'll be stuck within the confines of that denomination for the next five years, and you might never, ever fulfill the plan and the purpose of that which I have for your life."

And the hardest thing that I did was to take that letter and put it away. The hardest thing I did was to take that tape and not even make copies of it, but put it away and say, "Okay. Okay, God. Here we go." And then we ended up in a little church of 25 people in Warsaw, Indiana!

Evangelist Richard Moore was working for the ministry, and we were paying them a $100 a week. Richard, bless his heart, was supposed to do everything to help me, but he was the first person in the prayer line! It didn't matter what call I gave, he came up for it. I laid hands on him and he was out under the power. And then I had no help! Richard traveled around America with me, but he was on the floor more times than he was anywhere else!

We stayed two weeks in Warsaw, Indiana. And there's only one thing worse than one week in Warsaw, Indiana, and that's two weeks in Warsaw, Indiana! We might have even stayed three, but neither of us care to remember!

Now when we left Africa, I had a half-hour telecast on Trinity Broadcasting Network in the Ciskei area. Somehow, they contacted TBN over here in the U.S., and I got an invitation to go on TBN. I thought, *This is great. Praise God. Another break. This is the break we've been waiting for, hallelujah!*

I booked my flight out thinking, *I'm going to be on the program, "Praise the Lord," and it's just wonderful. Just what we've been believing God for.* I spent several thousand dollars to get out to California, to book a hotel, and to get a rental car.

Monday night, something came up at TBN and they said

they couldn't have me on the program. I thought, *God, what in the world is happening?* Tuesday went by, then Wednesday, and I was just in the hotel, stuck there by myself. Thursday went by and I thought, *I've wasted the whole week. I've wasted several thousand dollars that I didn't have. I'm spending money that I don't have to meet people I don't even know.* And then they called me and they said, "Look, you'd better come. It's not going to work out for you to be on the *Praise the Lord* program, but we can put you on a program called *Behind the Scenes*. I thought, *That's just phenomenal. That is just unbelievable!*

I was walking around the hotel saying, "God, what are You doing to me? I came out here. I've even told people that I'm going to be on *Praise the Lord*, and now, I'm not even on that. I'm going to be on *Behind the Scenes*. This is just phenomenal. We are really having a breakthrough, we are having a mighty revival—within a matter of four days, I've gone from, *Praise the Lord* to *Behind the Scenes*!"

Now, what I did not realize was that the Lord knew exactly what He was doing. I did not know that the program *Behind the Scenes*, which was about ten minutes long, would air five times over the weekends, and I didn't know that there would be several people who would be watching the program.

I remember when I was walking in the hotel, I said, "Lord, whoever calls me from the program, I'll go there. I don't care where the call comes from; I will go there." And from the program, I got a call from upstate New York, and I got a call from Juneau, Alaska.

I said, "This is just great. This is phenomenal. This is awesome. Honolulu? Hawaii? Orlando, Florida? No, they didn't call. None of these places called, but great—Juneau, Alaska, called!"

THE WIND IS ABOUT CHANGE

> *The Wind is not about comfort, the Wind is about change.*

I'm sharing this for a reason, because many times, when we talk about the Wind of God, we think it's all about comfort, but it's not. It's about change. The Wind is not about comfort, the Wind is about change.

And the thing I know about the Spirit of God is that He will not force you to change beyond what you can tolerate. In other words, if you say, "God, that's it. I'm stopping right here," He'll let you camp right there, and you'll stay there. Ten years will come and go, but you'll stay right there. He will love you and He will bless you, but you might not see all He has for you. You'll see a limited measure. He'll have wanted to do more through you and in you, but He couldn't do more because you said, "Lord, I have to stop now."

He is *so* gracious. I have known His graciousness, and even today, I know His graciousness. He says, "I'll wait for you. And when you're ready for more, tell me, and I'll come and do some more change."

So you go along, and two or three months later, you'll feel that Wind. You'll think, *What's that happening?* It's the Wind blowing again. You are feeling the Wind of the Spirit of God blowing, and you'll sense a change coming. You'll say, "Lord, change me, change me," and He'll say, "Okay. You seem ready now to go to the next level."

And people think, *Well, this is a once-in-a-lifetime thing, the same as when you are born-again—when you're born-again, you're born-again.* But it's not. The Bible says we are changed from glory unto glory (2 Corinthians 3:18).

There's a level of glory that I experience, but there's another realm of glory just beyond *that* realm of glory, and then there's another realm of glory just beyond *that* realm of glory. But I'm not going to experience that next realm of glory if I don't allow Him to change me into *this* current level of glory. You can't jump levels.

THE PRICE OF GOING TO THE NEXT LEVEL

There is a price to pay to go to the next level, and the price is upon your flesh and upon your mind—that's the price to pay. Many people talk about warfare and all that kind of stuff, and they think it's just about fighting devils. But it is about that thing right between your ears, called your mind and your flesh. Because the flesh hates lying on the altar.

As one person said, "The problem with a living sacrifice is that it always tends to crawl off the altar!" We may come to a service and sing, "Where He leads me, I will follow," and we may cry, "Yes, Lord, I will go." Then several boxes of tissues later we cry, "Lord, I place all on the altar." But afterwards, when we go out there and He starts working, we cry, "Don't touch that. Leave that alone. Stop! God, don't mess there." Then the Lord says, "But you said, 'I give you everything.' You said, 'I put it all on the altar.' Now, make up your mind, son. What do you want? Do you want it all on the altar, or do you want half on the altar?"

People cry, "I want the fire of God," and they get the fire of God, but they don't realize that the fire of God is going to come and burn everything that's not of God!

That's why when pastors say to me, "I want a revival in my church," I say to them, "Do you really want it?"

"Yes, I want it."
"No, you don't want it."
"Yes, I do."
"No, you don't."
"Why?"
"Because things are going to be different around here when the fire of God falls. Some of your plans and some of your programs are going to be burnt up. You'll say, 'Oh no. No, you can't touch that. I've been working on this for five years. We've had that vision . . .' But it wasn't God's vision, so it's going to burn. You can't call for the fire and then, when things start burning that you don't want to burn, put a hold on it, get the fire extinguisher, and say, 'Whoa, whoa, whoa! Let's renegotiate this level of commitment. Call 911!'"

TRUST THE WIND AND WHERE IT BLOWS YOU

You have to trust that God knows what He is doing. Now, following the *Behind the Scenes* program I also received a phone call from New York. It was a lady who sounded a little strange. I thought, *Great! God, this is phenomenal, a wacky woman on the phone!* She said, "We want you to come to upstate New York." I said, "Do you have a church?" She replied, "No, I don't have a church, but I know some people." I thought, *This is phenomenal. She doesn't have a church, but she knows some people. This is all I need!*

The other call was from Juneau, Alaska, and I asked the lady, "Are you a pastor of a church?" She said, "No, I'm not. But I know some people!" I thought, *This is phenomenal! I get two calls, Juneau, Alaska, and upstate New York, and they both "know some people." God, this is phenomenal. I've been "Behind the Scenes," and now they "know some people!"*

THE WIND OF GOD: PART ONE

Little did I know that the first call from upstate New York, would change our whole ministry. The move of God in our ministry broke out in America in April, 1989, from this phone call. The lady made the call to the pastor she knew, and when we arrived in April 1989, we were met by Pastors Paul and Caroline Tebbano. He had assumed I was black because I was from Africa, so he was shocked to see me. He said, "Well, where's Rodney?" I said, "This is me!"

When I spoke to Pastor Tebbano on the telephone, he said, "I want you to come and hold a weeklong series of meetings." And first of all, that was a breakthrough because most pastors at that time would not go beyond Sunday! Some would do Sunday morning, Sunday night, and Wednesday night, but I could never understand why nobody wanted to have a meeting Monday night. But at that time, I was not familiar with Monday Night Football in America!

Monday night in Africa is a night where everybody stays at home. It's just after the weekend and everybody is recovering after the first day back at work. Here in the U.S., it's a big night—Monday Night Football, with chicken wings and all that, but I didn't know that. So when I would say to the pastors here in the U.S. that we wanted to go Sunday morning, Sunday night, and Monday night," they would say, "No, no, don't do Monday night. Monday is not a good day." I'd say, "Why? Monday is a good day." "No, it's not a good day. Monday is not a good day," they'd reply. And I only found out later it was because they wanted to stay home and watch football!

So when Pastor Paul said, "I want you to have a weeklong meeting, Sunday morning, Sunday night, Monday, Tuesday, Wednesday, Thursday, and Friday," you can understand that I was so excited. My hand was shaking holding the telephone; then he said, "Can you do morning meetings also? Monday through Friday morning?" I thought, *I've died and gone to Heaven*!

I said, "You want me to do morning meetings too?" He said, "Sure. We'll tell the church to come, and they can get leave and vacation time, and we'll have a special time together." At that time, they ran about 250 people and they met in this little strip mall between a bar and a furniture store. We arrived there Sunday morning. Sunday mornings I always shared my testimony of how the Lord touched me in 1979, and the fire of God fell on me, and that Sunday morning we had a move of God. Then Sunday night, I started the series which I always did, on the gifts of the Spirit. For the weekday mornings, Pastor Tebbano said to me in advance, "What are you going to speak on, so I can tell the people to take time off work?" And I had said, "I'm going to speak on the subject of the anointing."

And so Monday morning, sixty people showed up. Now someone says, "That doesn't sound like a lot of people." But that was a lot of people to us at that time. That's sixty more than we had ever had in our lives before on a Monday morning, because we had never had a Monday morning meeting! Then Tuesday morning, a hundred people show up. I said to Adonica, "Something's happening! Because this is almost half of the church that are showing up on a Tuesday morning. Something is happening here." And as I was teaching on the subject of the anointing, just talking normally, the very atmosphere of the room suddenly changed.

THE WIND IS OUR AUTHORITY

Now my desire was always to preach twice a day, six days a week. And I thought that if I could do that, I would have died and gone to Heaven. I didn't care if anybody was there to listen, as long as I could minister twice a day.

I would buy my own tapes, listen to them, send myself an offering, prophesy to myself, encourage myself on a daily basis, and even write letters of invitation, inviting myself to preach in London, England! You have to do it when you're starting out because nobody else will do it. I would get with some preachers who'd say, "I have four hundred invitations to preach," and I'd think, *Oh, my God. I haven't had any invitations.* In fact, everybody I called to go and preach at their place said, "Just keep passing through," because they always say, "Whenever you're passing through, call." So I'd call and they'd say, "Just keep passing through!" I felt like, "Hit me again. I'm still conscious!"

When I started in the ministry, I didn't have papers or credentials. Everywhere I went they said, "Where are your papers?" I'd say, "I don't have any," and they'd reply, "Well, when you get papers, come and see us." Then when I had papers, I'd drive up to the church and say, "I have papers," and they'd say, "Now put them away. We don't need those things!" And I'd say, "But you never told me that two years ago!"

I remember one day sitting at the table, and I was so upset because I'd been turned down to preach because I didn't have papers. I said, "God, this is not right. I don't have any ordination papers. I've got nothing, and they won't have me if I don't have papers. God, I've got to have some papers. Lord, I need some papers." I thought, even a piece of signed toilet paper would suffice—I just had to have some papers!

And as I was sitting there talking to the Lord, suddenly, in a flash, I saw a certificate, and it said, "This is to certify that Rodney Morgan Howard-Browne has been ordained to the Gospel Ministry." It had all of the relevant stuff on there, and it had three signatures. It said, "Father," and, "Son," and "Holy Ghost!"

And that day, my life changed. So after that, when people said, "Have you got papers?" I'd say, "I've got papers."

"Can I see them?"

"I don't have them with me right now, but I can get them. It can be arranged. Where do you want the lightning to strike? Boom! 'This is God. Yes, Rodney Howard-Browne has papers!'"

JUST LET THE WIND BLOW

I love preaching, but I just decided that I really wanted God to move and touch the people. I saw preachers get up and work themselves into a frenzy, sweat and need towels, and need to have a shower after the service. They worked so hard to get somebody to pray for, and the B3 would be playing all the while. I'd think, *If they do two meetings a day, six days a week like that, they're going to kill themselves!*

Now there's nothing wrong with working hard like that, but you have to do it in a limited way, otherwise, you won't have a voice. At that time, I also sang and I didn't want to wreck my voice. So my prayer was, "Lord, what I'm going to do is just get up and speak the Word, and You do it. You want to heal the people, so You heal them. You want to touch them, so You touch them. I'm not saying I won't get involved, and I'm not going to say I'm not going to break a sweat, but I'd like to have a voice after forty years (because all the old-time preachers I grew up around didn't have a voice). I want to keep a voice. Please. I'll sacrifice everything on the altar, but just let me keep my voice."

I even knew preachers that blew their voice out and couldn't preach. That's a terrible thing, to blow your voice out and can't even speak.

THE WIND CHANGES THE ATMOSPHERE

So there I was in the morning service in upstate New York, just preaching on Luke 4:18–19, "The Spirit of the Lord is upon me, because he hath anointed me to preach the gospel to the poor; he hath sent me to heal the brokenhearted, to preach deliverance to the captives, and recovering of sight to the blind, to set at liberty them that are bruised, to preach the acceptable year of the Lord." And as I was talking along those lines, the very atmosphere of the room changed.

Now what do you do when that happens? Nobody can say that I was manipulating. I wasn't doing anything; I was just talking, and the atmosphere of the room changed. People started shaking in their seats, and some were falling out of the seats. Others were weeping. Others were laughing uncontrollably. And the crowd was diminishing, not *out of* the door, but *onto* the floor. And people were laughing.

Now I knew about the joy of the Lord, because I had seen my mother hit with the joy of the Lord when I was only five years old. She was hit that way for three-and-a-half hours, so I knew about that, but I'd never seen it like this. I'd never seen it on this scale—in a church, in the middle of the message. It's one thing when you've finished the message—"Every head bowed, every eye closed. Nobody looking around, believers in an attitude of prayer"—and then God can do whatever He wants to, but not in the middle of the message!

I hadn't finished preaching and they were getting touched. You can't say, "I haven't finished preaching. I've got a message here. You're ruining my tape series. I've got a special series, and I'm going point by point; then I'm going to the original Greek and the original Hebrew. I have seven points and three steps to the forty-eight ways, and then 900 different reasons, and there's a poem. So, I want it to stop, please. I want to read the poem!"

There were people all over the place, it was a mess, and I was standing there thinking, *My zipper is down.* Then I thought that maybe somebody had come up and pinned a donkey tail on my back or something.

Now when you're in a service and you're speaking, you expect everybody to be quiet. It's one thing to laugh at a funny joke, but it's another thing to keep laughing and then just fall out on the floor, hit your head on the pew, and roll on the ground under the pew. You think, *Hello. It's finished now. We've moved on from that. The joke is over. We moved on; we left that. It's actually not funny anymore.*

So as the minister, it's unnerving to you. I said to the Lord, "What are You doing? Lord, You are ruining my meetings." And the Lord said to me, "Son, where your meetings have been going lately, they are worth ruining!" But I remembered I had said, "God, come and do whatever you want to do."

At the end of that service, I called a line of people, I lined them up across the front, and I told them to join hands. I held on to the podium with my left hand, and I reached over the podium to grab the hand of the first person. As I did so, a Wind came from the side and blew the whole row out under the power. It buckled my knees, and I held on to the podium for dear life. And the move of God broke out.

By Friday night, we couldn't pack another person in there; we had more people saved and healed by accident, than when we had tried to get it done on purpose! The Wind blew in there!

THE WIND BLOWS YOU OUT OF YOUR PLACE OF COMFORT

> *It's not always in the place of comfort that we find the next step or phase of what God has for us. Sometimes, it's just in the place of obedience where we do what we don't really want to do. God watches your obedience.*

From that moment as a minister, I had to change. I had to forget about all my recordings and teaching series. Today, I'm able to put together some teaching series, but the Lord said to me, "Do you want the tape series, or do you want a move of the Spirit?" I said, "But Lord, I need the tapes," because in those days, I'd take four tapes, put a rubber band around them, and sell them for $10. And if I sold three tapes, I could get a hotel at Red Roof Inn for $29.90. Three tapes would pay for the hotel for the night, and an extra tape sale would buy hamburgers for the kids.

So you can talk about comfort and the comfort zone, but then you say, "Lord, I'll do whatever You want me to do. I'll go wherever You want me to go; just take my life. Take me." But it's not always in the place of comfort that we find the next step or phase of what God has for us. Sometimes, it's just in the place of obedience where we do what we don't really want to do. When you end up going to a little church that's struggling that tells you they can't even give you an offering and you say, "It doesn't matter; I'll come," God watches your obedience.

And then the next place unfolds, and sometimes, you look back over 12 months, and you say, "If I hadn't gone there, then that wouldn't have opened up. I wouldn't have met that person. That door wouldn't have opened." And in the next chapter, I will go on to tell you what happened in Juneau, because there's a long story about Juneau, and if I hadn't gone to Juneau, I wouldn't be in Florida today.

If you just look for the "Honolulus" and the "Waikikis," you will miss the "Madison Square Garden" and the "Cairo, Egypt." I tell you, it's being obedient to go to the Warsaw, Indianas; the Ozark, Alabamas; the Laconia, Indianas, with congregations of 65 people. It's uncomfortable I know, but remember that a pearl never comes forth until the oyster is irritated.

THE WIND LIFTS THE NAME OF JESUS

> *It matters not who knows your name, but if you allow the Spirit of God to birth that which God wants to do in you by the power of the Holy Ghost, they might not know your name, but they'll know His Name. And His Name is Jesus, and they'll know Him in the power of His resurrection.*

God will raise you up from obscurity. You might say, "Nobody even knows my name," but it has nothing to do with that. You can be used of God with thousands of people in the meeting, but they still may not know your name. One time when I was walking down the row in a church, a lady lying on the floor grabbed my pant leg and said, "Who are you? Who are you?" Because nobody had introduced me, I had just walked out and took over the service. They didn't know my name.

It matters not who knows your name, but if you allow the Spirit of God to birth that which God wants to do in you by the power of the Holy Ghost, they might not know your name, but they'll know *His* Name. And His Name is Jesus, and they'll know Him in the power of His resurrection.

I tell you, you are not reading this by accident. You are not a mistake and God has chosen you. And even if you are in a place right now where people don't receive you, just wait; something is going to happen by the Holy Ghost. It's much bigger than what you can see now. Something beautiful is going to happen, something that is going to last until eternity, because all God looks on is the heart. He looks on the heart. Praise God!

2

THE WIND OF GOD: PART TWO

Blown by the Wind to Do the Master's Bidding

John 3:8 declares:

> The wind bloweth where it listeth, and thou hearest the sound thereof, but canst not tell whence it cometh, and whither it goeth: so is every one that is born of the Spirit.

I love this verse of Scripture, because it helped me understand what happened to me at the start of my ministry, and why things happened the way they did. I had thought, *Lord, have mercy, something is wrong with me.* Then I stumbled onto this verse, and I really like the Amplified Version (Classic Edition) which says, "The wind blows (breathes) where it wills; and though you hear its sound, yet you neither know where it comes from nor where it is going. So it is with everyone who is born of the Spirit."

DON'T RESIST THE WIND

> *The Spirit of God is always moving, but He is not always moving the same way. You have to be so sensitive.*

You cannot dictate the way of the Wind. On the Day of Pentecost, the Wind of the Spirit of God blew with great power. It was, "a rushing mighty wind," (Acts 2:2). I want you to know that whenever the Holy Spirit comes into a place, it's still going to be the "rushing mighty Wind." He is not less of a Wind today than He was back then. And when the Wind of God blows, it brings change.

You and I can go with the change, or we can stay where we are. And many who were once touched by the Spirit of God and were raised up and used by God, today are stuck in the doldrums of religious tradition and going nowhere because they were not willing to change and make the adjustments.

If you are willing to change and make the adjustments, then the Spirit of God will take you onto the next thing which He wants you to do. Something about the ministry of Jesus is that He never showed up when He was expected to show up. Just ask Mary and Martha, who said, "If you'd have come out, our brother would not have died" (John 11:21 paraphrased). Jesus waited four days, and didn't even show up at the funeral. Then He went to the graveside and pulled Lazarus out of the tomb.

I know that might not sound too "pastoral," when you don't show up for the death of someone who's very dear to you, but Jesus was not going there to bury Lazarus, Jesus was going there to raise him up. Hallelujah!

THE WIND OF GOD: PART TWO

BE SENSITIVE TO THE WIND

> *You cannot dictate the way of the Wind. You and I can go with the change, or we can stay where we are. Many who were once touched by the Spirit of God and were raised up and used by God, today, are stuck in the doldrums of religious tradition and going nowhere because they were not willing to change and make the adjustments.*

You must be so sensitive to the Wind. One thing I've found out about the mighty rushing Wind of the Spirit of God is that He's always moving, but He is not always moving the same way. And you have to be so sensitive.

When you were a kid and you wanted to fly a kite, you'd go outside, wet your finger in your mouth, and then you'd hold your finger up to see which way the wind was blowing. Have you ever done that? I check which way the wind is blowing on the golf course. I bend down, take a tuft of grass, and throw it up in the air to see which way the wind is blowing. The tuft of grass goes one way, and then you know where you've got to aim the ball, and you know what club you've got to use. A lot of things are dependent upon the wind.

In this day and this time we live in, airplanes depend upon the wind. You can have a tailwind, or you can have a headwind. Sometimes, people are going against the Wind of God, and they've got a great headwind. But it's better to get into the flow of the Spirit of God and get a tailwind! I love a tailwind. There is nothing like having a Wind on your tail, moving you along, feeling that God is propelling you. The Spirit of God is blowing you and moving you into a place, and you don't really know all of what it is happening. You can't really put it down on paper. If somebody came to you and said, "Tell me exactly where we're going." You don't really know, because if you knew, it probably wouldn't be the Wind of God.

> *The Spirit of God is blowing you and moving you into a place, and you don't really know all of what it is happening. You don't really know, because if you knew, it probably wouldn't be the Wind of God.*

BE OBEDIENT TO THE WIND

John 3:8 says, "the [Spirit] bloweth where it listeth so is every one that is born of the Spirit." So you can hear the sound, but you can't tell where it's coming from or where it's going. Please understand, this is the Bible. So Abraham went out looking for a city whose builder and maker is God (Hebrews 11:10). God said, "Get out from your country" (Genesis 12:1), Abraham didn't know where he was going.

We say, "Lord, where am I going?" And God says the same, "Go!"

"Okay. Where am I going?"

"Just keep going."

"Oh Lord, please tell me where I'm going."

I shared in the last chapter how we had only been in America for under a year, and I was invited to speak on television on the program *Praise the Lord* on TBN. At the time, we had a half-hour weekly program called, *The Voice of Healing*. They heard about this program here in the U.S., and they invited me to come. So, I flew out to California. I spent several thousand dollars to fly (money I didn't have), paid for the hotel, and told everybody that we were going to be on *Praise the Lord*.

However, as I said earlier, they had postponed my appearance and by Wednesday, I had still not received the call. I thought I had wasted my money and my time. Then I got a call on Thursday, and they told me they were putting me on a program called *Behind the Scenes*. The *Praise the Lord* program ran several hours, and had they had me on the program, I'd have been on there for about twenty minutes, or maybe a little longer. I originally thought, *Great! Now I'm on a little ten-minute program!* But what I didn't know was it aired five times over that weekend. And one of the calls we got from the program was to go to upstate New York. And that's where the revival broke out in April, 1989, but the other invitation was to Juneau, Alaska.

At first I thought, *I'm even more behind the scenes than I was when I started,* but I shared with you in Chapter One how the revival broke out in upstate New York, and if I hadn't gone out to California to TBN and spent that money, we would never have gone to upstate New York. So now, let me tell you what happened in Juneau, Alaska. When I called the lady up, she said, "I know the pastor of the church down here," so she called him and he said, "All right. Get him to call me." So I called the pastor.

Now in the early days, people would always say to me, "Well, send me a cassette tape," and I really used to get irritated with that, because I thought, *Lord have mercy! What do they want me to send the tape for? Maybe I should ask them to send me a tape, so I can see if I really want to go and preach at their dead church!* Because it works both ways, *what do you mean, send me a tape? Here is the tape; I'm playing it right now—I'm talking on the telephone!*

BELIEVE IN YOUR MINISTRY

> *Get on the phone and book your own meetings. If you don't believe in your ministry, why should somebody else believe in your ministry?*

As an aside, I want to say this to any traveling ministries reading this: you can develop all your packages, your promotional materials, and your promotions, and send them out, but that's not where it's made. That's not where it's done. Let God anoint you to get on the telephone. Do you know how many times a pastor has written to me stating he was canceling the meeting? But then I have gotten right on the phone and said, "Pastor, can I ask you a question? What in the world are you doing?"

"Well, I feel we can't have the meeting this time."

"We have revival. My God. What's wrong?"

"Well, people have left the church."

"That's even more reason why we have got to have the meeting. We'll come and smack that thing up the side of the head, and we will have revival and run the devil out of Dodge."

"Oh, then you'd better come on then."

And the meeting that was going to be canceled suddenly has become a meeting again because I preached to him on the telephone. Don't have somebody else book your meetings like some booking agent who books a meeting here and books a meeting there. Get on the phone and book your own meetings. If you don't believe in your ministry, why should somebody else believe in your ministry?

You've got to believe in what God's called you to do. Jesus believed in the ministry that He had. He said, "The Spirit of the Lord is upon me, because He hath anointed me" (Luke 4:18). So, you have to get on the phone and say, "Listen, I'm coming to town."

In the early days, I had to literally convince the pastor that we would have revival. He didn't know me from a bar of soap. I'd say to him, "I promise you, we are coming to town and we are going to have revival." And I'd even say, "If we don't have revival, I'll give you all the offerings back." Well, they would take me up on that, and many of them prayed that I didn't have revival so they could get all the offerings back!

So I called the pastor in Juneau, Alaska, and the Lord really anointed me to speak to him. He was from a certain denomination, and you've got to know how to talk to the different denominations. If you get the Church of God on the line, it's, "All right, pra-ise God. A-men? Halle-lujah, yesss. A-men."

A Church of God preacher going through a drive-through will say:"Pra-ise God, can I have two cheeseburgers, and give me some of them golden fries, A-men." If you have got a charismatic on the line, just tell him you can have a foot washing service, and he'll book you! But I'm not against the denominations—we love people from all the different "abominations" or whatever.

Now the pastor in Alaska was really hesitant. He was not too sure and he said, "I don't know you." So I said, "Well, I don't know you either, so it's mutual, isn't it? But I really feel this was supernatural how this call came in." Anyway, the Lord hooked us up and we went to Alaska for a meeting.

Now Juneau's a small town, of probably 32,000 people, but it is actually the capital of Alaska. The first night, a woman got out of a wheelchair—the first night! This woman was one of the leading people who was known all over the town. And when you're in a town of 32,000, and somebody's prominent in the place, and has been confined in a wheelchair for, I believe it was, five years, word is going to get out. She climbed out of the wheelchair, and the buzz went throughout the whole city. We ended up staying there three weeks, holding two meetings a day, Sunday to Friday, and people came out of the woodwork. They flew in from all the little islands round about.

We estimated that probably close to 20 percent of the population in that little town, was affected by the revival. You could go to the airport, and they were talking about the meeting. You could go to the supermarket, and they were talking about the meeting. So there was a buzz!

MAKE ROOM FOR THE WIND TO BLOW

> *If you book yourself up in advance, you can book yourself out of the move of God.*

The way I operated at that time, was that I never booked up in advance. I always kept my calendar clear, with like four or five churches on the side. I wanted to have revival, and if you book yourself up in advance, you can book yourself out of the move of God. You can book yourself up. Somebody says," I'm booked up for five years." But I say, "Well, great! Phenomenal! But can God even get onto that schedule?" There's nothing wrong with having things organized, but remember, the Spirit blows where it listeth (John 3:8).

The Lord has given me the ability to look at the calendar, and I'll say, "That crusade we are planning two months, three months from now, I'm unhappy about it, and we need to cancel it." You can ask Pastor Eric Gonyon, and he'll verify I'm telling the truth. I'll look at the diary, I'll look over the weeks, and I'll say, "I'm unhappy about that meeting. That meeting is not of God, get that thing off the calendar. Cancel it."

And I learned that, because in the early days when I went ahead and had the meeting, it was a disaster, and I knew. So, I learned. Even an old pig, if every time it goes down to drink at the trough, a brick falls on his head, after a while it will get the revelation, *Drink water, brick, pain.* So you learn after a while! And I can look at the calendar and tell you, "That's not going to be a good meeting." I've had a meeting scheduled for later in the same month, but I've canceled it. Listen to me carefully: if you have to push to make things happen, things will start to go wrong. Some people interpret it as the devil, but I don't. We say this in our ministry: "If you have to force something, it's not God." Because when the Lord makes a way, He parts the sea. Now I know the difference between when the enemy is trying to stop it and when God doesn't want you to go. There's a big difference. So I keep the calendar clear.

Then, when I was at a church, I would always say to the pastor, "Do you have a brother, or cousin, or uncle in the ministry? Or is there some other place you could recommend us?" Because you need a break into new areas and territories. You can't just keep going to the same churches over and over and over, otherwise, you become part of the furniture. And then the people become familiar with the anointing, and they don't place a demand on it. That's why I tell pastors, "You need to travel out, even if it's just once or twice a month, just to stir your ministry, because you can sit within your church and die. The people become familiar with you, and you become familiar with the people. And then, they don't place a demand on you as the pastor, and you won't place a demand on them.

But if you travel out, you always come back fired up when you know people are drawing on the ministry. If you don't draw on the ministry, you won't receive anything. If you don't place a demand upon it, you will not receive a thing."

If you have to force something, it's not God.

TRUST THE WIND, AND DON'T TRY TO WORK IT OUT

You must place the demand upon the anointing.

There are some places I just won't go back to, but, not because I don't like them. I do like them, but they need to get somebody else in there. It's just I've been there, seen that, done that, bought the T-shirt, and sold the T-shirt to defray expenses! You must place the demand upon the anointing.

Sometimes people want you to stay, but that's the time to leave. And sometimes when they want you to leave, that's the time to stay. Someone says, "I think you should shut the meeting down." But you say, "Oh, that's wonderful. You want me to stay longer?"

"No. I said shut the meeting down. We should end the meeting now."

"Oh, you mean, we should carry it on for another three weeks?"

And then other times it's: "Please stay."

"No. I actually need to quit. We'll finish Friday night."

"Are you crazy?"

"No, the Wind of God is moving me."

Everyone born of the Spirit will be blown by the Spirit. The

THE WIND OF GOD: PART TWO

Spirit bloweth where *it* listeth, not where *you* listeth! You can blow *with* the Wind of the Spirit, or you can blow by yourself, and I'd rather stay with Him.

So the Alaskan pastor referred me to another pastor, and when I called this pastor, he said, "Listen, we are out of Fargo, North Dakota." I thought, *This is just great: Fargo, North Dakota. I needed to hear this. Juneau, Fargo, upstate New York. These are all places where there's snow and ice and blizzards. Lord, do You really love me? Other ministers, are blessed. I hear they are in Hawaii all the time, doing a conference, and I'm going up to North Dakota!* So, I went and preached in Devil's Lake, North Dakota. "Devil's Lake" of all places!

But we had a great time there in 1992. Eight hundred men packed the church, and the power of God shook that place. What God did was just awesome, and it affected the whole state of North Dakota because the men came, and their lives were changed. People on their way home were falling out in restaurants. Two guys who had driven independently to the meeting, went to the same restaurant to use the restroom. In one stall, the door was closed, but one of the guys was on the floor, laughing uncontrollably inside the stall. The other guy was in the next stall and was also laughing. One said to the other, "Where have you traveled from?" He replied, "I've been up there at Devil's Lake." The other guy said, "Yeah, I was up there at Devil's Lake too," and the power of God hit them.

So we went to Fargo, and revival broke out. We were probably there in Fargo three or four weeks, and then one of the men came to me and said, "I'm a chaplain here in the prisons. Can you come and preach in the prison?" I was doing two meetings a day as it was, and I thought, *This is great. Now I'm in the prison in North Dakota. Phenomenal!*

I preached in the men's facility, then I preached in the women's facility, and I rushed over to get back to the church to preach that night. After the service, the pastor said to me, "Listen, would you come and hold a meeting for my brother? He has a church in Michigan." I thought, *God, this is great. This is still north, and freezing cold.*

I said, "What's the name of the place?" He said, "Mount Pleasant, Michigan." Now, I never asked people how big the church was because it didn't matter how big the church was. I'd always say, "How many can you seat?" I probably should have asked how big their churches were because some had big churches, but they didn't have many people.

So I just said, "How many can you fit into your church?" He said, "I think we seat close to 300." I thought, *That's fine; we will go there.* Now, I had to go back to Africa to preach first, and the Lord was really beginning to do some great things back in southern Africa. We made trips back there almost like Holy Ghost terrorists going in. We would launch back in there, drop a Holy Ghost "bomb," and leave before they could do anything about it. We would go back every six months, and we'd come in like terrorists, and boom! Then we'd just leave. We didn't stay too long because we'd have gotten killed. You have to follow the Holy Ghost—follow the Holy Ghost!

So to make a short story even longer, I came out of South Africa where we had close to 4,000 people and standing room only in the meetings. I jumped on a plane and flew straight into New York and then on to Michigan. I landed, and we walked out Sunday morning in the church, and there were 30 people. Just 30 people! Thirty people in "Mount Disappointment," Michigan.

I looked at Adonica and I said, "What in the world? My

God, we've missed the Lord! We're in trouble here. Thirty people?" And then I just said, "You know what? I've never run from anything. We're going to smack this thing up the side of the head every which way but loose, bless God. There might be only 30 people now, but we're going to have revival. Either that, or we're going to have a riot! This will either be known as the great Mount Pleasant Revival of 1992, or it'll be known as the great Mount Pleasant Riot of 1992. I'll either die here, or we will have a move of God."

We just swung the bat every which way but loose that night. I think we had 18 people Monday morning. I was still leading all the worship on the keyboards, and when you have 18 people in the meeting, it doesn't take that long. You get up, you lead the worship, and they look half-dead, so you think, *Well, that's not going to work,* so you shut that up. Then you preach, and they don't even receive that. Some places you go preach, people look at you, and you wonder if they even understand you. They speak English, you speak English, but you feel like you need an interpreter! You stand there speaking, and you feel like you can't really even go into the deep things of God, so you just stay with the basics—"Jesus loves you. He really does. You are special to Him. 'Jesus loves the little children, all the children of the world. Red and yellow, black and white, they are precious in His sight. Jesus loves the little children of the world'" (C. H. Woolston and George F. Root).

The meeting started, and it was over by 12:00 noon because I had laid hands on them four times already. After all, it was only 18 people: "Fill, fill, fill, fill," and we were finished.

I was thinking, *I'm ministering here, but look at the previous week in South Africa. My! What glory! We had the place packed out. People were hanging on the rafters, and now here we are with eighteen people. Boy, we are at the "jumping-off" place.*

That week, I had to subsidize the offerings myself. I had to put money in just to encourage myself. My wife came to me saying the offering was phenomenal. I said, "I know. We put 90 percent of it in ourselves!"

And I went back to the room I was staying in, and I began to write the book *The Touch of God*. I spent the next four weeks in revival in Mount Pleasant, Michigan, and writing the whole book, *The Touch of God*. Little did I know, that that would be the last opportunity I would even have the time to write for probably the next four or five years.

There I was, grumbling, moaning, and writing *The Touch of God*. But by the end of the four weeks, the place was packed out, with over 300 people. People were hanging off the walls. It was a move of God, and the Lord blessed them.

So I came to the end of the final week of the meetings, and I had no clue where I was going to next. Friday night, a pastor walked up to me and said, "Here's my card. I have a church north of here. When can you start?" I said, "Sunday morning. I'll be there. I'll be there this Sunday morning." He said, "Are you kidding me?" I said, "Look, you asked me when can I start, and I'll start Sunday morning." He said, "But we don't have time to announce." I said, "That's even better."

I said, "How many people do you have in your church?" He said, "I have about 150." I said, "That's fine. Do they all show up on Sunday? We will have revival." So, we packed up on Saturday, headed north, and arrived at the church. The same thing happened there, except that within a week-and-a-half, we had to get a 600-seat tent, and we had to move outside of the church into the tent. Then the tent became packed. Now I was thinking, *Thank God I came to Mount Pleasant. It wasn't pleasant, but it's pleasant now.*

Some things aren't pleasant, but become pleasant later because God has to take you through there. And while I was there, not only did I write a book, I picked up a worship leader, and I didn't have to lead worship anymore.

> *Everyone born of the Spirit will be blown by the Spirit.*
> *The Spirit bloweth where it listeth, not where you listeth!*
> *You can blow with the Wind of the Spirit, or you can*
> *blow by yourself and I'd rather stay with Him.*

THE WIND WILL BLOW YOU FROM PLACE TO PLACE

So we were in this tent meeting and the pastor said to me, "Do you think you could go down and have a meeting for my brother?" And I was waiting for the announcement of the city—I thought it was going to be Duluth, Minnesota, or somewhere similar. He continued, "Could you go down and hold a meeting for my brother down in Stuart, Florida?" I thought, *Florida? Florida? Yay! Thank You, God!*

I didn't even have to pray about it. I had been confined to the frozen wastelands of the North for the previous three years, and I just went into emergency tongues, I was so overjoyed. I said, "Sure." So, I got on the phone and called him up. We finished the meeting we were in, and Adonica had to drive down with the kids. I jumped on the plane Saturday, and went straight down to start the crusade. In fact, Adonica left two days earlier, so she could be on time. We got into Stuart, and guess what? We arrived, and heading straight for us was Hurricane Andrew!

I had been waiting for years to come to Florida. I'd been praying for years to come to the state of Florida. Now the Lord had opened the door, and we had a hurricane! And Hurricane Andrew turned out to be one of the worst Florida had seen for many years. It was coming straight for us. We had to evacuate twice from the place we were staying. I had never seen a hurricane, and I wanted to see one. I kept going outside to look, "Where is this thing?"

I was praying for the thing to hit us because I thought, *My God, we're going to have a hurricane. This is awesome. It's not every day you have one.* The pastor said to me, "You don't want to have a hurricane." But I said, "Yeah, we want to have one." So, he said, "Well, if we have a hurricane, we can't have a revival." I said, "What do you mean? Of course, we're going to have a revival."

The pastor said, "We'll have to cancel the meetings." I said, "We're not canceling anything. I didn't come here to cancel our meeting." He said, "There's a hurricane coming in. They reckon it's going to be one of the worst we've had in years. We have to cancel." But I told him, "We will not cancel this meeting. We are going to have this meeting."

Because you don't understand my background. When I was a kid, we had a flood in the city of Port Elizabeth. It was so bad that the water was flowing up to the door handles, and everybody stayed at home. We lived 17 miles from the church, but my dad loaded us up in the car and we went to church. People were going by the car in a motorboat! There we were, the Howard-Browne family driving down the road, and there was a motorboat going past us!

But my mom and dad had a commitment—you go to church! In all the years growing up, I can never remember missing a service. We were there Sunday morning, Sunday night, Wednesday night, and Friday night. Saturday night, there was a prayer meeting at our house, and we were always there. So even in the flood, my parents were going to church. And I thank God for my dad and mom because they set the pattern and the standard for our life, and put God first.

In the end, Hurricane Andrew didn't hit us. It was about 90 miles away. And really, we didn't even have a gale force wind. It just kind of looked like a rainstorm to me, so I was a little disappointed. I thought we'd really get to feel it. However, when I saw what it did to Homestead, Florida, I really thought, *My God!*

So that was the weekend the revival broke out in Stuart, Florida, August 1992, and it picked up momentum. And again, within two weeks, we were in a tent and that packed out. And God, through that door, opened the door for us to come into central Florida, Carpenter's Home Church, in Lakeland.

THE WIND BLOWETH WHERE HE LISTETH

I met with Pastor Strader in December 1992, and we came to Lakeland in March 1993. Now, let's trace those steps back: If I hadn't gotten on a plane and flown out to California, spent my money, and got on *Behind the Scenes*, I'd have never gone to Alaska, which would not have opened the door to North Dakota, which would never have gotten me into the prisons to preach to the prisoners, which would not have taken me to Mount Pleasant, which would never have taken me to Lakeland. The wind bloweth where it listeth (John 3:8).

I remember, around 1991, we went back to Pastors Paul and Carolyn Tebbano from Clifton Park, New York, and we were there a week. I was scheduled to go to the Bronx of New York to a large church, but on the Friday before, the pastor called me up and said, "Don't come, we are having a mighty revival."

I thought, *That's crazy. Don't cancel the meeting on the last day. If you give a month, you can at least make some arrangements. Don't just cancel.* And I want to say this to pastors: Don't just cancel people. And if you do, give them the offering they would have gotten if they were with you and bless them, because that's how ministers live. Traveling ministers live on the road. Don't just cancel them, think nothing of it, and send them $100. Think twice before you book somebody.

I said to Pastor Paul Tebbano, "I don't even know where I'm going." I had my mom and dad with us at that time, several other people, and of course, all the kids. We were due to check out of the hotel Saturday morning before 12:00 noon, so I got an extended checkout. You say, "Why?" So I could try to find out where I was going. My mom called, and when your mom calls you, you have to have some answers.

And my mom knew how to get answers out of me. If you needed to get ahold of me when mom was still alive, you just called my mom, and trust me, she'd have gotten ahold of me. She'd find me anywhere on the planet. She'd call me any time of the day or night, and she would come up with the answers. Nobody else in this ministry could come up with the answers like my mom could. Thank God for moms. My mom was the number one interrogator. She should have been working for the CIA and the FBI.

So my mom called me and said, "Where are we going, son?" I said, "Mom, I don't know, but just give me a little while and I'll tell you," and I put the phone down. I got another call; it was the other people traveling with us, "Where are we going?" I said, "I don't know. Trust me. We'll have a place."

At 11:50 a.m., the phone rang. It was a minister out in California, and I told him about my predicament. He said,

"Listen, where are you?" I said, "I'm in upstate New York." He said, "I've got a friend in a place several hours from you. It's also in New York. Call him up. Maybe you can go there."

So, I called this pastor up, and he was kind of rude on the phone. He said, "Well, I don't know you." I said, "I know you don't know me. I've just been up here and we've had a great move." He said, "I've heard a little bit about it, and I'm not too sure if I really like what I hear." And he said, "How do you operate?" I said, "Well, we always we pay our own expenses and we receive a love offering." "Well," he said, "I'm not sure if I'm really open to that either."

I said, "We run Sunday to Friday."

"I don't want you to do that. Just do Sunday morning."

I said, "I don't do Sunday mornings." I said, "I run Sunday to Friday."

"Well, you just do Sunday morning and then we'll see if God moves. If God shows up, then we'll carry on."

I said, "What do you mean? God might not show up tomorrow morning? Then maybe I don't want to come if God's not going to show up."

So he said, "All right. Come on down anyway." I put the phone down, we checked out of the hotel, and I said, "Everybody, come on. We're heading down to this town called Hyde Park, New York." We got down to Hyde Park, New York, and the pastor looked me over, checked me up and down, and interrogated me. We went into the Sunday morning service, and the power of God hit the place. It was like a wind. Do you know, we stayed three-and-a-half weeks at that church? We held two meetings a day, and 2,500 people in the Hudson Valley were touched by the power of God. Hallelujah!

THE WIND BLOWS ON OPPOSITION

I'll just tell you one more quick story. We were in Spring Hill, Florida, back in January, 1993. That meeting ran four weeks, and the power of God hit the place. I believe it was written up in the *St. Petersburg Times*. Miracles were happening! One day, we had seven instant miracles just on the way to the parking lot. The service had finished, and on the way out of the door to the parking lot, people were getting out of wheelchairs and off crutches. And I said, "God, that was great, but it would have really helped us if those miracles had happened in the service." Because then we had to try to convince people we had seven miracles on the way to the parking lot. You could imagine them thinking, *Yeah, right. Produce some miracles now, buddy.*

Then I got a call from Brisbane, Australia. And a minister was over there in trouble. "Can you come and help immediately?" And this was right at the height of the revival in Spring Hill, where the place was packed. I think we crammed close to 800 people in their building—you could hardly move. But the minister said, "Could you come and help?"

They said getting a visa would take seven days, but I got one within a day, and we were on a plane headed straight into Brisbane, Australia. We arrived at this tent and started preaching there. It was located opposite an Assemblies of God church who brought in an evangelist to run an "opposition revival," so that it wouldn't affect their church. The tent was there, so they wanted to have an "opposition revival!" Churches do that. They hear about what guys are having, and then they book another meeting at the same time, to run an opposition meeting.

I know you may not believe this. Maybe you're shaking your head, thinking, *My God. This cannot be true. You are making it up now.* But guess what? The evangelist who came in to do the opposition revival, finished his meeting and heard about the tent meeting. So he came over to see what was going on and when he walked into the tent, the power of God hit him. He ended up under the anointing, with his head right by one of the big tent pegs. He was really drunk under the power of God. I gave him some of our videos. His name was Tim Hall, and he is now my dear friend. Tim took the videos, made copies of them, and distributed them all over Australia.

In Brisbane, I'd been in this tent that was around 120 degrees, and I didn't drink enough water. I had gotten dehydrated in the tent, and then got on the plane to fly home. By the time I landed in Oklahoma City, my kidneys were struggling. I was going to do a conference for the North American Indians, where all the different tribes were coming together for a whole conference. It was the first time in the history of my ministry that I could only preach two or three days. I said, "Look, I have to go. I can't even carry on. I can't even get out of bed. You take over the meeting." I had never at that time done that before. I said, "I must go because I've got this meeting starting Sunday in Lakeland, and I need to go and just get some rest." And I walked right out of the Oklahoma City meeting, and I landed in Florida and took two or three days' break. Then I walked right in, and smack-dab, it was like a Holy Ghost atomic bomb went off in central Florida.

But fast-forward now to January, 1995. We went back into Australia, and God gave us some of the greatest revivals and moves of God, with arenas packed out with 12,000–14,000 people, from Perth to Adelaide to Melbourne to Sydney to Brisbane, even up to Cairns on the Great Barrier Reef—all because those videos had gone all over Australia. And when I arrived in Perth, Western Australia, there were 6,000 people packing out an arena. I said to them, "How many have been in one of the meetings?" Nobody raised their hands. I said, "How many have seen a video?" And everybody raised their hands. All because an "opposition revival" was held opposite the tent meeting, and a man came in and fell out under the power, with his head stuck there by the tent peg. Glory to God!

LET THE WIND TAKE YOU WHERE HE WANTS YOU TO GO

> *Don't criticize another man's ministry. Don't judge another man's calling because it was the Wind blowing him there. It was not blowing you there; it's taking you another way. Just do what the Master says.*

So don't look at your life and say, "This was a success. This was a failure. Maybe I shouldn't have done this, and I shouldn't have done that." Hook up with the Wind of the Spirit of God, and let the Lord blow you. Let the Lord take you where He wants you to go. There'll be times you don't understand why God's leading you a certain place. There'll be times when the Lord tells you to join yourself to this chariot, and you get to preach to the eunuch (to an individual) (see Acts 8:26–40). And you'll think, *God, I'm just here on the chariot, preaching to a eunuch.* But then He'll send you into the city. Philip preached to the eunuch, and then he went and preached in the whole city, and there was great revival in the city.

Whether it was the masses, crowds or individuals, He was preaching to, it didn't bother Jesus. I know in America everybody's worried about the crowds. Listen, the crowds followed Jesus when He had the loaves and the fish, but when He said, "Unless you eat my flesh and drink my blood . . ." (John 6:53), the crowds left. And when He went to Calvary, He went alone. So if you're going to be motivated by crowds, you're really going to have a problem. Crowds come and crowds go!

I'm not against crowds, God's blessed us with great crowds, but it's not about crowds. If it was about crowds then surely the Day of Pentecost would have recorded that 30,000 people showed up, but that didn't happen. It was only 120 people who showed up on the Day of Pentecost, yet we are still reeling from the impact of that revival and that move of God today.

Whether it was the woman at the well, or it was the people on the mount, Jesus said, "I'm about the will of my father. I'm doing the will of my father. I'm doing what God wants me to do" (John 6:38). People come and say, "What are you doing?" But don't criticize another man's ministry. Don't judge another man's calling because it was the Wind blowing him there. It was not blowing *you* there; it's taking you another way. Just do what the Master says. Do what the Lord says to do.

So don't look at your life and say, "This was a success. This was a failure. Maybe I shouldn't have done this and I shouldn't have done that." Hook up with the Wind of the Spirit of God and let the Lord blow you. Let the Lord take you where He wants you to go.

RUN WITH THE WIND OF HEAVEN

You've got to find out what God wants *you* to do, and then run with the Wind of Heaven. You must not compare yourself to others. Comparing yourself to others is so dangerous because when you start to compare yourself with other people, and you start to look at other ministries, you will try to do what they do and follow where they go, trying to hook up with the Wind. But you've got to find the Wind of God for yourself. And there will be times when everybody seems to be going one way and you're going the opposite way. Then, the tendency is to think, *Maybe I should be going the other way?* But the Lord will say, "No. *This* way."

It's a lonely thing, as far as people are concerned, but it's not lonely with the Holy Ghost. It is only lonely where people are concerned because people are people and they change opinions daily. Someone said to me one time, "Brother Rodney, they don't like me." I said, "They don't even like themselves. You should have heard the fight they had with themselves this morning when they got out of bed."

The Apostle Paul said, "Preach the word; be instant in season, out of season" (2 Timothy 4:2). There are times when it's going to be out of season, so what do you do? You preach the Word. *Preach the Word!*

JUST DO WHAT HE WANTS YOU TO DO

> *It's about doing what the Lord wants you to do. You can put a meeting together anywhere, anyplace, anytime, but whether God shows up in the meeting, is another story.*

I only want to do what the Lord wants me to do. I'm not really interested in a big meeting or some big crusade. I've had all those things. I've got photographs. We've got photo albums coming out of our ears. I can take you back and show you hundreds and thousands of hours of videotapes of meetings. We've had great meetings around the world, but that's not what it's about. It's about doing what the Lord wants you to do. You can put a meeting together anywhere, anyplace, anytime, but whether God shows up in the meeting, is another story.

This is significant for what God is wanting to do within the framework of our ministry here in Tampa, Florida, because the Lord has actually brought us full circle. During the pandemic and for the months after, we were right back to the place where our calendar was pretty much cleared. We have "The Stand" every night, and our annual conferences, but I'm talking about me traveling around the world. However, in 2023, God opened extraordinary doors on a level that we have never seen before and countries are once again opening up for me to travel to. The Wind is blowing us in with huge opportunities to speak to presidents, leaders, and even kings. But it is the Wind blowing us. We have not sought to do it ourselves. The Wind is going before us and blowing us there, and the Wind will blow us back from there, and onto other areas and countries.

There was a time when I kept the calendar clear, so I could get the mind of the Spirit for what God wanted me to do. And there was always that element of surprise. When you announce too far ahead, when you come in to the place, the devil's waiting for you. When you don't tell anybody, the devil doesn't even know you've been in town until you've had the revival, and there's really nothing he can do about it.

BECOME A MYSTERY AS THE WIND GUIDES YOU

Stop trying to analyze yourself and make sense of yourself. The more you hook up with the Holy Ghost, the more of a mystery you are going to be.

That's why years ago, I never really advertised that we were going to Egypt. I never called certain magazines or certain people in certain areas, trying to get on TV, announcing we were going to Egypt. I kept quiet about it. I purposefully told everyone not to say anything about it, and not to mention it. We talked in our church, we prayed, and we interceded here at The River, but we didn't tell anybody because the more people that had known about it the more problems would have been created. So we kept quiet about it. And when the Lord sent us in there, it was like a Holy Ghost bomb was dropped in the land of Egypt. One thousand people were saved in Cairo, Egypt. And while I was standing on the platform, the Lord said, "I want you to come back here." Now, if we had been booked, I would have had to say, "Lord, I'd like to, but we can't; we've got somewhere else to go."

And following Egypt, we had invites to Havana, Cuba, and Baghdad, Iraq. Things that I had been praying for. Let me say this to you: Stop trying to make sense of yourself. Stop trying to analyze yourself and make sense of yourself. The more you hook up with the Holy Ghost, the more of a mystery you are going to be. And the more you yield to the Spirit of God, the more of a mystery you are going to be. There'll be days when you'll wake up and the Lord will say, "Get in your car." You'll get in the car, drive down the road, and you'll ask, "God, where am I going?" And He'll say, "Just drive down the road." There'll be whole days like that, and God will lead you and supernatural things will take place. And at the end of the day you'll say, "What a supernatural day this was. Oh, hallelujah."

There are things happening right now that I cannot even tell you about publicly. There are things I can't even share with you regarding doors and opportunites that God is opening up and places the Lord's opening up for us to go. You'll hear about them later. But don't put God in a box. Follow the anointing and follow the Wind. Follow the Wind of the Spirit of God and great shall be the results.

YIELD TO THE WIND

> *The Master is looking for those who would yield themselves unto the Spirit of grace, who would allow the Holy Ghost to fill them, who would be blown by the Spirit here, and blown by the Spirit there, to do the Master's bidding.*

I feel the Wind, I feel the Wind of Heaven blowing right now. Hallelujah!!

> Change, change, change, change. There is coming a change. There is coming a change; you've sensed it for quite a while. You've said, "God when shall it be?" It's even now at the door. Don't be afraid; fear not; it's for the good, and you'll step up higher into the next realm of what I have for you. Change change, change, change, change.
>
> (PROPHETIC WORD)

You can sit around, and you can format a plan. You can write it down on paper, and you can try to plan ahead. And then there are certain things you'll feel a check in your spirit about. And maybe even people around you will get excited about a project and say, "We're going to do it." And then you'll have to come back to them and say, "You know what? We're not going to do it."

"What do you mean, we're not going to do it? Why are you changing?"

"Well, I know we've talked about it, but I feel a hesitancy in my spirit, and until I know why I feel the hesitancy, we can't even go there."

And then you'll wait just a week or two, praying in the Holy Ghost, and you'll come back and you'll say, "No, we can't go that way. God will not allow me."

In Acts 11:12 we read, "The Spirit bade me go"—the Holy Spirit said to go, and other times, we read that the Spirit was restraining (Acts 16:6). So, we are are restrained by the Holy Ghost, or we are released by the Spirit of God. We cannot be people filled with the Holy Ghost and do what *we* want to do. We *cannot* do what we want to do. We have to do what *He* wants us to do. Our life is not our own. We are bought with a price (1 Corinthians 6:20).

The Master is looking for those who will yield themselves unto the Spirit of grace, who will allow the Holy Ghost to fill them, who will be blown by the Spirit here, and blown by the Spirit there, to do the Master's bidding. The Spirit of God is looking for men and women in this day and this hour who will lay down their own agenda, who will lay down their own plans, purposes and their own ideals, and say, "Lord, I yield myself to You. Where do You want me to go? I'll do what You want me to do, and I'll say what You want me to say. Not my will, but Thine be done."

DON'T RESIST CHANGE

That's why God is going to raise up a whole generation of young people, because many times, people get too old and mature, and get stuck in their ways. They say, "I'm not going to change," and are obstinate. "I'm not going to change. I've done it this way for years." But God says, "I want to do another thing with you. I'm going to break you out of your comfort zone. I'm going to pull you out of your comfort zone. I know what I'm doing with you. My plans for you are better than your plans for you. So, what's your problem?"

Do you think the Lord's going to let you down? He won't let you down. Do you think the Lord's going to fail you? Someone says, "But I'm worried about the future. What about our retirement and our provision?"

Listen: David said, "I have been young, and now am old; yet have I not seen the righteous forsaken, nor his seed begging bread" (Psalm 37:25). The Bible says, "If ye be willing and obedient, ye shall eat the good of the land" (Isaiah 1:19).

DON'T BE MOVED BY WHAT YOU SEE

Trust the Holy Spirit. I don't care what it looks like in the natural. I don't care if things don't look like they are working out like you think they should. Trust the Holy Ghost.

Sometimes, people do things out of fear for their future and preservation for themselves and their family. Let me tell you right now, "They that trust in the Lord shall be as mount Zion, as a city that cannot be shaken. As the mountains surround Jerusalem, so the Lord surrounds his people" (Psalm 125:1–2, paraphrased). I just feel the anointing of the Spirit of God on that!

You don't want to get to Heaven and have the Lord say, "Come back here. Let me show you what could have happened if only you had just yielded to Me." I know I don't want that to happen. I want the Lord to say, "What I wanted and what you did was right-on, son."

I didn't know what God was going to do when we went to San Diego. When I met Dr. Mark Spitsbergen, he had rimmed glasses on, a big beard, hair all over the place, was wearing sandals and shorts, with his shirt hanging out, and he was drunk under the anointing of the Holy Ghost. He said, "Will you come to San Diego?" I looked and thought, *My God, who is this guy?* He was a rancher, a filmmaker, and a lot of other things. I've never found anybody like him—he wears fifteen different hats! He learned five Bible languages, and you name it, he's doing it.

I didn't have a problem with him, but I just looked at him and I thought, *Oh . . . okay*. But when we went into San Diego, several thousand people showed up for the crusade, and the power of God hit there. And that was really when the Lord hooked us up together. There's no telling what the Lord's going to do in the days to come, but if I'd have been moved by what I first saw of Dr. Spitsbergen, I could have missed that. Just be careful you don't miss your day of visitation. I have the highest respect for Dr. Spitsbergen. He's a man of God, with a great wife, family, church, and ministry and I have the greatest fun with him. I take him around all these doctors of theology, and I turn him loose. They shut up because he knows more than they do. All these great Greek scholars fall so quiet. I just tell them that he has learned five Bible languages, and that's it—they say nothing.

Trust the Holy Spirit. I don't care what it looks like in the natural. I don't care if things don't look like they are working out like you think they should. Trust the Holy Ghost.

What if your name is Noah and you're building an ark? "But

Lord, I've been preaching for 120 years. I've got a boat. There's no water. I've got seven other people in the boat with me. We don't even really get on that well ourselves because we're family and I've also got a bunch of animals." You just have to trust the Holy Ghost!

PREACH WHAT YOU HEAR THE WIND SAY

> *I went away from New York with the message the Lord had given me, that the storm was coming, and "What would happen if a missile struck New York City?" But everybody looked at us like we were crazy. "What do you mean a missile striking New York City? What missile strikes New York City? Please!" But I was just preaching what I heard the Wind say. I heard the whisper of the Wind say it, so I said it. I said what the Wind said.*

When we went to New York for the Good News New York Crusade, people thought we were crazy. "Rent Madison Square Gardens for six weeks? Are you nuts? Who do you think you are? You are not Billy Graham." I said, "I never said I was Billy Graham. I'm Rodney Howard-Browne. How can I be Billy Graham? The Lord spoke to me in a dream."

When we went there in July 1999, the first night we started in Madison Square Garden, we had about three thousand people. People thought it was a failure, but that was a great crowd for Manhattan in anybody's language. Even in German, Greek, and Italian, that was a great crowd for Manhattan. You try going to Manhattan and getting a crowd together!

The crowds grew to three, four, five, six, seven, and eight thousand. By the last week, we turned away 5,000 people!

Forty-eight thousand people were saved, but I just knew that's what God told us to do. And I went away from there with the message the Lord had given me, that a storm was coming, and "What would happen if a missile struck New York City?" But everybody looked at us like we were crazy. "What do you mean a missile striking New York City? What missile strikes New York City? Please!" But I was just preaching what I heard the Wind say. I heard the whisper of the Wind say it, so I said it. I said what the Wind said.

Someone says, "Who told you?" A Wind told me. I walked away from there, and I even had people call me and say, "You were just a failure. That thing was a flop. You are a failure." I even thought I was a failure. I thought, *I know God spoke to me in a dream, but in the natural, it does look like a flop.* I said, "God, it doesn't look like we were a success." And do you know what the Lord said to me? He said, "I didn't call you to New York to be a success. I called you to be obedient." Then September 11, 2001, happened, and the Twin Towers fell—boom! And then, I had such relief knowing we had obeyed the Holy Ghost.

And God said to me, "What about the Cross?" Churches put on Easter plays and get 10,000–15,000 decisions over Easter. But when God put on THE "Easter play," there were maybe only two decisions—the thief on the cross and the centurion. A church will put on the "Via Dolorosa," a live donkey comes on, a camel poops on the platform, and 10,000 people get saved. But Jesus did the *actual* Via Dolorosa, and only got two people saved. But was the Cross a success? Of course!

Then let's just talk about the Old Testament prophets. How would you like to be an Old Testament prophet who prophesies, but you never even live to see your prophecies come to pass?

Then 400 years after you are dead, what you said comes to pass, but you actually died thinking, *I'm a flake.*

Then what about Pentecost? Only 120 people in the Upper Room. Was that a success? Of course!

Churches put on Easter plays and get 10,000–15,000 decisions over Easter. But when God put on THE "Easter play," there were maybe only two decisions—the thief on the cross and the centurion. That was it! But was the Cross a success? Of course!

FOLLOW THE WIND

I feel the Wind of God as strong today as I've ever felt it in my life, and something awesome is about to happen, and it is involving nations of the Earth. It is not even about cities anymore. This is not even about local churches anymore. This is about nations being shaken by the fire of God Almighty. Hallelujah!

Stop judging things by the natural. Follow the Wind of the Holy Ghost. Follow what the Lord is telling you to do.

I'm going to tell you one of the things the Lord said to me when we first came to America. The Lord said to me, "Find out what everybody else is doing and do the opposite, and it'll be Me! Whatever's happening in the Church, do the opposite, and then it will be Me, son." That's what the Lord told me.

I feel the Wind of God as strong today as I've ever felt it in my life, and something awesome is about to happen, and it is involving nations of the Earth. It is not even about cities anymore. This is not even about local churches anymore. This is about nations being shaken by the fire of God Almighty. Hallelujah!

> *Stop judging things by the natural. Follow the Wind of the Holy Ghost. Follow what the Lord is telling you to do.*

3

THE NECESSITY OF THE ANOINTING:

PART ONE

Learning the Ways of the Wind

> The wind blows (breathes) where it wills; and though you hear its sound, yet you neither know where it comes from nor where it is going. So it is with everyone who is born of the Spirit.
>
> JOHN 3:8 (AMPC)

One of the greatest problems we deal with today in the modern-day Church, is that they've lost the ability to discern, or have sensitivity to the anointing of the Spirit of God. And because they've lost the sensitivity to the anointing of the Spirit of God, people forge ahead without Him.

I can't tell you how many times I've been to meetings where

they've told me what the program is for the meeting, or what kind of program they want. It's all laid out, and you know exactly who's going to do what, almost at what time. But I see nothing there scheduled for God and for the Wind to blow in the Church.

> *One of the greatest problems we deal with today in the modern-day Church, is that they've lost the ability to discern, or have sensitivity to the anointing of the Spirit of God. And because they've lost the sensitivity to the anointing of the Spirit of God, people forge ahead without Him.*

BE TOTALLY DEPENDENT ON THE HOLY GHOST

> *We are in constant need of revival. Revival brings us back to our first love, brings us back to our first works, and brings us back to the place where the fire once burned.*

We have to be *totally dependent* upon the Holy Spirit. After all, the Holy Spirit is the One sent to the Earth by the Head of the Church, the Lord Jesus Christ, to help us. Apart from helping us in our personal and private lives, being our Comforter, Intercessor, Standby and the One called alongside to help us in everything that we need on the Earth just to live in victory, He is also the One Who helps us minister. So I ask you, with tears in my eyes, "How can we minister without the Holy Ghost?" How dumb can you get and still breathe? You've got to be smoking some bad religious weed to think that you can even be a minister outside of the Holy Ghost!

I heard one man say, "I know it's a move of God, but I don't want it in my church." I don't think he even realized what he said. You wonder what kind of a church he was running—a nightclub? A bowling alley? A bingo hall? You must understand, it's not about what *we* want, it's what *He* wants!

A lot of people don't understand what religion is all about, and they don't understand what tradition is all about. Now, not all tradition is bad. There is good tradition—like when you cross the street and you must look left and right—that's good tradition! Or don't take a bath with your hair dryer plugged into the wall, that's a good tradition. But Religion is a terrible thing. Religion is any ritual you do in the Kingdom of God over and over again without any results, or without any reality or substance to it. Communion can be a ritual. The laying on of hands can be a ritual. And it's so easy to fall into rituals. It's so easy to get into a rut (and remember, a rut is a grave with the ends kicked out!).

That's why we are in constant need of revival. Revival brings us back to our first love, brings us back to our first works, and brings us back to the place where the fire once burned.

I remember a minister telling me that God had really blessed him and given him a great revival. The church had exploded to over 10,000 people. We were in discussion one day, and I was remarking about the early days, when the power and the glory of God really used to be in manifestation. He said, "Well, you have to understand, that was just when we started. We've kind of matured now, and the anointing has become more administrative." But he was really trying to make an excuse for the fact that the anointing of God was not in display. And he was trying to say that people were babies at that time, so they needed the power of God. But now, they were more "mature."

THE WAYS *of the* WIND

But I thought, *Lord, have mercy! Just slap yourself up the side of the head!* How do you move on from the Book of Acts? How do you move on from the Holy Ghost? You have to learn the ways of the Wind.

> *If you go to a place and He's not blowing, then something's wrong. You missed Him somewhere, and you'd better get back to the place where He was once blowing. God's always been moving, and He's never stopped moving.*

STAY WITH THE WIND

You must learn the ways of the Wind and stay with it. If you are a pilot, you will know it is important to learn the ways of the wind, and you know you have to watch it constantly. You have to find out what kind of headwind you are flying into, so you can put enough fuel into the plane so you can land. It's the same with the Spirit of God.

There's not anyone reading this who can go outside and by your breathing, create a wind strong enough to blow down a tree. Likewise, we can't bring the Wind because the Wind is of *God*. But we can flow with the Wind of the Spirit, and He blows where He wants to. If you go to a place and He's not blowing, then something's wrong. You missed Him somewhere, and you'd better get back to the place where He was once blowing. God's always been moving, and He's never stopped moving.

I've been in the ministry since 1980, and now, especially in revival, I get amused with people who come to give me an opinion about what has been going on in my ministry. Yet the last time they saw me, it was one year ago. It's the funniest thing.

THE NECESSITY OF THE ANOINTING: PART ONE

They don't know the ways of the Wind.

When the revival first broke out, we had every Tom, Dick, and Harry come. And do you know, the revival is of a greater intensity today than it was in 1993? We might have had 10,000–15,000 people coming to check it out, but we had a bunch of "looky-loos." People who never got touched, but just sat there and looked, *blink, blink*. They saw people fall out on the floor and they yawned, and then got up and walked out of the door. They went to the restroom and came back, and then checked out the service a little more. They weren't really *in* the meetings, they were *at* the meetings. We had big crowds, but they weren't all *in* the meetings. They were just there. You can get wax dummies that do the same thing. The people never gave in the offerings, so you might as well have had a wax dummy sitting there. I laid hands on them, and it was like laying hands on a refrigerator! They didn't receive anything, and they didn't come expecting anything.

And we've had some preachers who showed up to meetings and conferences just to play golf afterwards. They don't come for revival because they don't flow in revival normally. Some of them are so bound up by tradition, and they are addicted to their denomination. They do not know the ways of the Wind.

MOVE WITH THE WIND

Now the Word is full of types and shadows. In the Old Covenant, when the children of Israel left the land of Egypt, they had the pillar of cloud by day, and the pillar of fire by night. That's a type of the Holy Spirit. They had to watch the Cloud, (you can read about it in Exodus 13). And when the Cloud moved, they moved.

It didn't matter how settled they got, they had to move.

Someone could have said, "Oh, not again. We just got here last night." But it didn't matter. They might have only arrived the previous night, but the Cloud was moving, so they had to move with it. And you have also got to move with the Wind of God. If you don't move with the Wind of God, you're going to be left behind. Many have been left behind wondering, *What is God doing?* People ask me, "Brother Rodney, what's God doing? What's God saying?" I think to myself, *What are you talking about? He's doing the same thing He's always done. He's saying the same thing He's always said. What are you doing and what are you saying?—That's the question! It's not what God's doing and what God's saying; it's what you're doing and what you're saying!*

People think God's not doing what He's always done because *they* are not doing what God wanted them to do. It's not because *God* stopped, it's because *they* stopped.

IT'S ALL ABOUT YIELDEDNESS

> *The very thing that stops you from yielding, stops you from functioning in the fullness of the anointing that God has for your life.*

Why do you think the Bible tells us to stir ourselves up in the Holy Ghost (2 Timothy 1:6)? It's because there is a place in your life where you can get settled in the Holy Ghost, and you have to constantly stir yourself up in the Holy Ghost. There is constant pressure from the outside—phone calls that take place just before you walk onto the platform, your dog commits suicide, your goldfish have a divorce, all kinds of crazy things happen. Then you are distracted and end up dealing with all of these things. And if you're not careful, you won't stir yourself up in the Spirit of God. You won't yield yourself to the Spirit of God, and you won't be led and controlled by the Spirit of God. God is looking for individuals who will totally yield themselves unreservedly, in total abandonment to the Spirit of God. The bottom line is that all this book is really about is *yieldedness*.

The very thing that stops you from yielding, stops you from functioning in the fullness of the anointing that God has for your life. Sometimes, you see an individual who is quiet and dignified get a breakthrough, and just jump out on the floor. The power of God hits them, and they dance in the Holy Ghost. Then afterwards they say, "I'd have never done that before. Something happened. Something broke. I'm just feeling a new freedom and a new liberty." And the full outworking of that is going to take place over the next months, as they walk in the new liberty they achieved in the Holy Ghost.

The Bible says, "Where the Spirit of the Lord is, there is liberty" (2 Corinthians 3:17). There is freedom, there is joy, and "in thy presence is fulness of joy; at thy right hand there are pleasures for evermore" (Psalm 16:11). Amen.

Every time I've said, "Lord, I want to see more; I want You to do more in the ministry," He's said, "Then I'm going to have to do it in you." So pastors, if you want revival in your church, *you* have to personally have it. You say, "I want it for my church," but sorry, you've got to get it for *you*. If your church gets it and you don't, it'll be the worst thing that could happen. The last thing you'll want is for your church to get revival and you don't have it because you'll be most miserable. *You've* got to get it. It starts from the head. Dead head, dead body!

BE CONSTANTLY DESIRING MORE OF GOD

You have to maintain your hunger, your thirst, and your passion for the things of God. I'm not talking about hype. I'm not talking about working yourself up into a frenzy. I'm talking about your heart, and the hunger, and the desire of your heart, for more of God. You must always be crying out.

When I was in Holland several years ago, I had a man come to the meeting who works with YWAM (Youth With a Mission) in Europe and was the director over that whole area. He knew me from when I was 13 years of age. And even at that age, I was involved at a high-level in that group. We sat down over breakfast and he looked at me and said, "Rodney, you haven't changed one little bit. You are still as radical and as wild as you were back then." I don't know what he expected. Maybe he expected me to have lost that fire and that passion because I've been in the ministry so long and traveled all over the world? But he said, "You are still the same."

However, I'm a lot wiser now, and I've learned a lot of things. Some of them have cost me quite a few million dollars to learn! What an expensive lesson it is when you learn in the school of hard knocks! Maybe you have a diploma or a certificate from the school of hard knocks yourself? But we change and we learn. It may take a while, but we do learn, even if pain has to be our teacher. It's just that some people have gone numb, so they don't even feel the pain now! But you have to keep that fire, that passion, and that hunger for the things of God.

> *You have to maintain your hunger, your thirst, and your passion for the things of God. You must always be crying out.*

TRADITION MAKES THE WORD OF NONE EFFECT

The thing we need to pray for is the fire of God to consume us. Firstly, to burn out the fear of man and secondly, to burn out the doctrines of men, the doctrines of devils, and the traditions of men. And then, we need to get Heaven's imprint on our hearts.

In Matthew 15, the Pharisees came to Jesus—the Pharisees, the Sadducees, the Couldn't-sees, and Wouldn't-sees. The Pharisees said, "Why do thy disciples transgress the tradition of the elders? For they wash not their hands when they eat bread" (Matthew 15:2). How terrible—the disciples just grabbed the bread without washing their hands!

Jesus said, "Why do ye also transgress the commandment of God by your tradition?" (v. 3). In other words, the Pharisees were more worried about the tradition, yet *they* were using tradition to transgress the commandment of God!

Mark 7:13, ". . . making the word of God of none effect through your tradition." I'll emphasize that: "making the Word of God of *none* effect because of your *tradition*!" People don't realize they do this also. They say to me, "Well, we've always done it that way. That's what we do around here, but we need revival Brother Rodney." Then when I walk in, I say, "Well, you better quit doing *that* and quit doing *that*," and they reply, "Oh no, we can't stop that. That's a little thing we do around here." And I reply, "Yes, but it's not bringing results, and you are making the Word of God of none effect. What part of 'making the Word of God of none effect' do you not understand? The Word of God is pure. You can't take any old thing, mix it with the Word, and expect to see Bible results. You cannot hold onto your traditions and make the Word of God of none effect."

There are a lot of sincere people in the Body of Christ, but they are sincerely wrong. They love God with all their hearts, but they are wrong. You can't get up and preach what *you* want to preach. The reason why the Lord has blessed us with a move of the Spirit, and we've been able to sustain it, is because of the Word that we preach. If we changed our message, the anointing would wane and we would not see results. Because if a parrot grabbed ahold of what I'm talking about, and the parrot just spoke these principles out from his cage every day—"Hey, you've got to get hungry. You've got to get hungry. You've got to get thirsty. You've got to get thirsty. You've got to press in to God. You've got to press into God,"—all the other birds in the neighborhood would have revival because the Word of God is spoken. There are certain things you have to have, period! Someone says, "Well, I just don't understand it." That's because they've got to learn the ways of the Wind. You have *got to learn* the ways of the Wind.

Jesus said, ". . . making the Word of God of none effect through your tradition." Oh, how many times have people done that? How many times have we taken the traditions of men and made the Word of God of none effect? That's why the thing we need to pray for is the fire of God to consume us. Firstly, to burn out the fear of man and secondly, to burn out the doctrines of men, the doctrines of devils, and the traditions of men. And then, we need to get Heaven's imprint on our hearts.

> *The Word of God is pure. You can't take any old thing, mix it with the Word, and expect to see Bible results. You cannot hold onto your traditions and make the Word of God of none effect.*

THE NECESSITY OF THE ANOINTING: PART ONE

WHAT IS REAL TO YOU WILL BE REAL THROUGH YOU
God will take the branding iron of fire from Heaven and put it on our hearts. Then, we will walk according to the pattern burnt on the inside of us. At all times, we follow the ways of the Wind of the Spirit of God.

You can always judge your message and what you have preached, by the level of the anointing. It will be one of two things: either you are just saying what somebody else said without believing it, without living it, and it not being a reality to you; or it is a reality to you. And it must become a reality to you because when it's real *to* you, it'll become real *through* you. The Holy Spirit can only become real *through* you as He is *to* you. The healing power of God can only become real *through* you as it is *to* you. The fact that God wants to bless you and prosper you, can only become real *through* you as it is *to* you.

I've had people come to me and say, "I teach all the stuff you do on giving, but we don't get anything." I reply, "Do you know why you don't get anything? You might use the same scripture. You might even use some of the same stories, but you don't live it, you ugly thing. It's not a reality on the inside of you!"

Many times I've heard somebody say, "We teach it just like you do," but I think, *You might teach it like I do, but you don't believe it like I do—I believe it!*

If you grabbed hold of some people and got in their face, under that pressure, they'd back off, about what they're teaching, and they'd change their theology right in front of you. I love to rattle people's cages. I just grab them and—boom! I hit them with an argument and I watch them backpedaling. You've got to *know* what you believe. Otherwise, when you start preaching it and you look out there and see some faces arguing with you, you'll start arguing with yourself!

> *God will take the branding iron of fire from Heaven and put it on our hearts. Then, we will walk according to the pattern burnt on the inside of us.*

THE MOVE OF GOD IS NOT TRANSFERRED BY OSMOSIS

You've got to know what you believe, and it must be real to you. You must stay in the move of God and with the Wind of the Spirit. Look at the early Church. What was the "early" Church? Was it a church that met at six o'clock in the morning? Some people think that, but there again, some people think that the Epistles were the wives of the Apostles!

People refer to the early Church "fathers" and when they say this, they are talking about people from the second and third centuries. But these weren't the early Church fathers. They might have been the early Church's great-great-great-great-grandsons, but they were not the early Church fathers. The early Church fathers were really the apostles and Paul. Anybody who came on after that had nothing to do with being an early Church father. In fact, only God knows what was going on in the second century. Things were probably so corrupted and so far removed from the move of God like they are right now. If I know religion and tradition, then probably within 40, 50, 60, or 70 years of the outpouring at Pentecost, the churches were already whacked and far from the Wind of God.

Please understand, the moment Paul died, it was the same as the moment any of the greats died. The next person comes to carry it on, and then the next person after that. But the move of God is not transferred down by osmosis. It's not transferred down by, "Hey, my father or my grandfather drove Smith

Wigglesworth around. He was a taxicab driver, and drove him around when he came to our town. So, I've got the anointing."

No, the move of God is not transferred that way. This became a reality to me on a trip to Zion City, Illinois. At the turn of the previous century, there was a man by the name of John Alexander Dowie. Now one of the things Dowie did was to found Zion City, Illinois, and he was the general overseer of the Christian Catholic Church (which had nothing to do with the Roman Catholic Church; rather, it meant the universal Church). Zion City, Illinois, basically grew to around 15,000–20,000 people who came to live there from all over the place.

Dowie had a phenomenal miracle ministry and was arrested over 100 times for practicing medicine without a license. You can understand how things were pretty strict in those days, as there must have been all forms of "quackery" going on. So when Dowie came along to town and miracles were happening, he got arrested.

God used him in a phenomenal way but nonetheless, in the end, he was in error and believed he was Elijah come back—which obviously he wasn't! But Dowie had such a gift of faith on his life that one time, they were on a train trip from New York back to Illinois, and as they passed through an area that had a drought for over three-and-a-half years, he said, "To show you I'm Elijah, it'll rain." And it did rain, and the drought broke. Another time he jammed New York City up for four miles with the sick and caused an upheaval. He had a phenomenal healing and miracle ministry. Now the ends of some of these ministries were not good. Because if you are not going to walk in accordance with the Word, if you get lifted up in pride, if you allow bitterness to come into you, if you open yourself up to false doctrine, or you don't walk according to the Scriptures, you will open yourself to immorality or whatever, and then the enemy will take you out. Period!

No matter how great the man or the woman is, no matter how great the anointing is, the enemy does come. Jesus even said to Peter, "Satan has desired to sift, you as wheat" (Luke 22:31 paraphrased).

So the enemy will come, and especially if you have an anointing. He'll take you out if you don't have an anointing, but if you have an anointing, he'll want to stop the anointing, and he'll do anything in his power to do so.

But John G. Lake came out of Zion City, Illinois, as did F. F. Bosworth and Lillian B. Yeomans. Gordon Lindsay's father and mother came out of that and Aimee Semple McPherson was affected because of it, and many other people were affected. Zion City really had an impact on the early Pentecostal movement in the 1920s and 1930s, because people get birthed in something, nothing just "happens." There's always something that is the cause. For example, look at Elijah and Elisha. What was Elisha's request? He asked for a double portion. Did he have it? Yes, because he had twice the miracles that Elijah had (2 Kings 2).

Someone says, "Well, it has to be with the call of God." Yes, but the desire has to be there. The desire comes to lead you to the call. The Bible says, "Covet earnestly the best gifts" (1 Corinthians 12:31). So if you desired a supernatural ministry, you could get it.

Now there are those who say, "Well, you know, God will sovereignly choose you," and all that kind of stuff. And I do believe in the sovereignty of God, but not to the point of, "Well, you can't really help it. God has not sovereignly chosen you, so then there's nothing left for you my dear friend other than to just hang around the fringes." I believe all these things in the Holy Ghost have been made available to us. I believe that

THE NECESSITY OF THE ANOINTING: PART ONE

with all my heart. And it has to do with the heart, consecration, and holiness—which you don't hear much talked about today. People don't like to talk about holiness. And holiness is not wearing your hair in a bun and not wearing makeup. You don't have to frighten people while you preach the Gospel!

But in the early 1990s, I was up in Illinois and I said to the pastor I was with, "I want to just go and check where Zion City, Illinois, is." So I took a rental car and drove up there. When I arrived at the campus they escorted me around, and the guy who is now the general overseer met me. We walked around and I was very interested in Dr. Dowie. The general overseer took me into the boardroom and there in the corner of the room was a portrait of Dr. John Alexander Dowie. Underneath, it read, "John Alexander Dowie, General Overseer of the Christian Catholic Church," and had the dates from and until. Then I found his successor, and I looked at his portrait. Then I looked at his successor and then I looked at the successor after that, all the way down to the guy standing next to me. And I said to him, "Tell me, do you guys pray for the sick around here?"

He said, "Well, we don't have the gifts of healing like Dr. Dowie had, but we do have a once-a-month anointing with oil." I thought, *It's just 90 years later and they don't pray for the sick here anymore? Ninety years ago, the walls were lined with crutches and wheelchairs, and braces, etc. But in a period of 90 years, whatever fire was there, has now gone. It's finished. It's over!*

So that's why I made the statement about the early Church fathers in the second or third century. They weren't fathers. They were no more fathers than most of the people running around churches today who call themselves fathers. They might be somebody's father, but some of them don't even know who they are father to!

WITHOUT THE WIND, THERE WILL ONLY BE A FORM OF GODLINESS

So now, if you take any great ministry on the Earth today and give it 50 years, what will be there? In fact, most revivals don't even last ten years. Because it's one thing when you are persecuted and attacked with all hell breaking loose in the middle of all Heaven breaking loose, but people get tired of that. And then they try to conform and become acceptable.

I don't want to mention names, but I've studied different denominations. If you go to the root of particular denominations, you'll find they had an explosion of revival at one time. But if you look to the person in the pulpit of those denominations today, you would not even link in your mind how he could have come from where he came from. The only thing you have to say is that the Wind left a long, long time ago and the person preaching is upstream in a canoe with no oars. He has a form of godliness, but denies the power thereof (2 Timothy 3:5).

The great Methodist movement took place because of a man by the name of Wesley. And of course, they've rewritten the history and they've gotten hold of all of Wesley's stuff, taking out everything that is of the supernatural. People do that. I can show you where there were great men and women of God and today, their children are rewriting their books, altering what their father said to make it more palatable. If I mentioned the names of these ministries, you would know them by name. It's because the children do not have the same fire the parents had. And the children would rather carve out for themselves an easier path than their pioneering parents did. The fathers were people who blazed the trail, who cut the path for you and I to be where we are today in the Holy Ghost. But the kids are not prepared to pay the price. They

THE NECESSITY OF THE ANOINTING: PART ONE

reap all the benefits, but they're not prepared to pay the price.

Daddy blazed the trail and didn't have enough money to buy tires, but the kids have got cars coming out of their ears and they have the audacity to pick up Daddy's book and rewrite it, still with his name on it. I tell you, I have more fear of God than to touch the anointing. If I did, I'd do it with fear and trembling, and if ever a storm or lightning came up, I would be down in a shelter!

I have a fear of God such that I would not even touch that which the Spirit of God has given to great men and women of God. I wouldn't touch it. I wouldn't touch it with a ten-foot pole.

WHAT WE DO MUST HAVE SUBSTANCE

Salvation is transformation. It's a radical change, and we need to have a substance to that.

Now the early Church had *substance*. They had substance to what they did and this is lacking in many churches today. Take a simple topic like salvation. I went back to southern Africa to a very large church of one of the main leaders in the nation. I preached on Sunday morning, and the place was packed. I think we had close to 6,000 people there. I gave an altar call, and at least 3,800 people responded. I don't know the full number, but I would say over 60 percent of the people stood up, got in the aisles, and moved forward. The pastor was angry and said, "They have misunderstood you." I thought, *Hey, I'm a South African and they are South Africans. It can't be my accent.*

So I said, "Okay, people. Please sit down. Bow your

heads, close your eyes," and I gave the altar call again. "If you are not born-again, and you don't know Jesus, if you died today . . . ," and this time, 75 percent of the people stood and came forward. And I looked at him, and he looked at me, and he knew better than to say anything. Do you know why that happened? Because the church had been growing, but nobody had given an altar call in probably five years. And if they did, they didn't have any anointing to do it. I have an anointing to give an altar call. When I start giving an altar call, if you are not saved, it is going to be like a giant vacuum cleaner. You are coming to the altar, I can feel the suction. I've even seen preachers sit with white knuckles probably thinking, *Maybe I need to go forward.*

In the early days, Evangelist Richard Moore traveled with us, and there were times when he'd say, "I think I need to answer the altar call." I'd say, "Richard, sit down and shut up." That's how it was, he'd feel the pull of the anointing. When God has anointed you to give an altar call, people just start running. They start coming out and it freaks the religious people because they don't understand what you did to get those people to come forward. But it's the Holy Ghost drawing the people. They are hearing the cry of the Spirit of God coming out of your voice. And people have to hear the cry of the Wind coming out of your voice.

But today, salvation in many churches is, "Does anybody want to get saved? We will throw in a week's vacation in Hawaii. If you get tongues, we will throw in a rental car!" It's like joining a club! A person will get saved, and then tithe out of their crack cocaine sales because there's been no change in them. In some churches, the devil is the usher, Judas is running the finances, Thomas is on the board, and Ananias and Sapphira are in the choir. The seven sons of Sceva have a gospel group, Goliath works in the parking lot, and the woman with the spirit of divination is the head intercessor!

Salvation is NOT a light thing. Salvation is the greatest miracle that can ever happen. And that's not saying that because we have the greatest miracle of salvation, then we don't need the others. That's the excuse of our Evangelical friends who say, "Well, He said, 'These works shall you do, and greater works than these shall you do' (John 14:12), and so, salvation is a greater work." Yes, that's true. But He also said, "*These* works shall you do." So even if salvation was a greater work, then let's at least have some of "these" works too.

But salvation is transformation. It's a radical change, and we need to have a substance to that. Otherwise, we are going to get the church filled with a bunch of reprobates. They are just people who sit and take up space, and they bring passengers with them! You walk out there, and as you look at them, you can see the "lights are on, but nobody's home." You can see the elevator doesn't go all the way to the top floor. You can see they are a hamburger short of a Happy Meal and that they have "passengers." The early Church had casting out of devils, but the modern Church has counseling of devils—the devils go for counseling:

"I need counseling,"

"What's your problem, Beelzebub?"

"Well, I'm a homosexual, and I'm having a problem."

"Well, if I can schedule you to come and see me for the next 30 weeks, we can walk through this together."

So, you spend the next 30 weeks with a homosexual devil. No wonder you're tired out; no wonder you're worn-out; no wonder you feel drained—you are counseling devils! Here's the bottom line, you ask the person, "Do you want to be free?"

Then you cast the devil out of them. There are homosexual churches now. There is a big church in Dallas who are advertising as such. So if you don't cast out devils, you're going to have all the problems, because the devils are coming to church! And where are they coming in? They are coming in through the people. Devils are holding them captive and whenever you preach, the people can't even see the truth. The devils are sitting there blocking the people's ears. While you are preaching, the devils are sitting there putting fingers in the people's ears saying, "Lalala. Lalala. Lalala."

So a person leaves the service and they never heard a word of what you said. And if you did shake hands with them on the way out, they'll tell you, "That was a great message." And then when they tell you what you preached, you'll think, *My God, did I say that?*

The early Church cast out devils. When people got saved, they got *saved*. When people got baptized in the Holy Ghost, they got more than just a language, they got the fire of God. When they laid hands on the sick, something actually happened. But today, you don't have to have anything happen in America to have a healing ministry. You just lay hands on people, and even if nothing happens, it is fine.

Evangelist Richard Moore said when he started the ministry, he preached for years and had "miracle and healing meetings" with no miracles! So that's point proof of what I'm talking about. But then God touched him, and now, he has phenomenal miracles. When God touches you, that's when you can move into that realm. That's when you can move into that dimension.

Do you know of churches where they lay hands on people, but nothing happens? It's because empty hands are being laid on empty heads. The hands of those who are coming to lay hands on people are empty, and the heads of the people coming are empty. But that's what religion requires! Religion requires that we do religious things. So people say, "Well, that's just what we do. You know, we don't see any results, but we do it. It's required of us. I've got to go to church today—the early service—so I can get out and we can spend the rest of the day at the beach. We'll just take an hour—the Hour of Power." And it's three hymns, three hers, take up the offertory, preach from the *Encyclopedia Britannica*, the *Reader's Digest*, and then pronounce the last rites. And everybody goes home just as dead as what they came. People sing, "Nearer, My God, to Thee" (Sarah Flower Adams, 1841), and you think, *Oh God, let it be today!*

People have to hear the cry of the Wind coming out of your voice.

THERE MUST BE EXPECTATION
There are ministers who come in, and they don't expect a thing to happen. And you have people come in, who also don't expect anything. And everyone leaves happy because they got what they expected—nothing! If you come to a service at The River expecting nothing, you'll get it. You can leave rejoicing, saying, "Praise God, I went down to The River at Tampa Bay. I went expecting nothing and I got nothing, I'm so happy!"

There must be *substance*—salvation, healing, and baptism in the Holy Spirit. Now what about water baptism? Do you know how many places we go where water baptism is like an afterthought as they dismiss everybody, and they just dunk people in the tank? At The River, we have big services where we put a swimming pool out, put seven people in at one time, and get them to raise their hands. I don't even get in the tank.

I just stand outside and say, "Now!" And the power of God knocks them under the water. We fish them out and stack them all over the place. You have got to expect God to meet people in the water baptism tank.

Salvation is powerful and so is the baptism in the Holy Spirit, but what's water baptism about? Just getting wet? No! It's a circumcision of the mind. It's a pulling back of the old carnal nature, allowing the new life of Christ to come through. It doesn't save you. Water baptism doesn't even clean you. That tank gets dirty after a while, and that's why I tell people after about an hour, "Close your mouth when you go under." But our water baptism services are powerful, full of fire.

Now what about communion? It should also not be an afterthought, "Quickly hand out the wafer and hand out the cup." Do you know the reason I think so many people are trying to find something more, something outside of what they see? It's because what they're doing doesn't mean anything to them. I get so excited when somebody gets saved. I don't have to see gold dust appearing on somebody's forehead. I don't have to have someone come forth and blow the shofar. I'm looking for the anointing, and I don't need somebody to come blow a horn. In fact, that's an irritant to me. "Get that thing out of here. You're messing up the presence of God, get that thing out of here." It's all about the presence of God.

I remember when we were in our previous building, a guy showed up one day with a shofar. I didn't know who he was. He was a visitor and didn't belong to our church. When you're a visitor, don't bring your paraphernalia with you. When you visit a place, don't bring your tambourine with you.

I watched him and I said to one of the ushers, "You go back there and whisper in that man's ear and tell him that if he so much as blows that thing, or even looks like he's going to blow it, I will insert that horn where they won't even get it out medically!"

About 20 minutes later, the power of God hit the whole place, and guess what? He took his shofar and started blowing it. And "shofar" we've never seen him again! Somebody says, "Why would you do that?" Because I have an obligation to protect my flock.

These people don't come so much in the morning services, they always come at night, because Pharisees are like false teeth—they only come out at night! Another time, we had a lady walk in pulling a golf cart. In the cart was an array of flags, and I sent the same message back to her: "Don't even think about waving one of those flags." It wasn't even ten minutes later she took her golf cart and off she went. Now you may think I'm being mean, but I'm not obligated to let everybody who just thinks they want to come in here, to come in here. It's not, "Have demon, will attend."

That's why we have the signs up at The River that say, "Right of admission reserved." Because I have to keep The River religion-free and tradition-free. I have to in order to protect the anointing. If I accommodate Brother Shofar and Sister Flag, then I've lost the anointing.

And in any event, what'll happen anyway is that they'll come to our church, get involved in the fabric of the ministry, and then get irritated by something else I say, maybe on giving. Then they'll infect 50 people and suck them out of the church. So hey, let's just hit it right up front, while we can. This is going to be painful any which way we look at it, but it's better painful now than later.

Some people say, "Well, that just goes to show that you're

not really a pastor. I wouldn't do that. I have a *real* pastor's heart." But my reply is, "Oh, so you pastor devils as well. My, what a great pastor you are! Phenomenal pastor! You pastor devils and demons under the guise of a pastor's heart." No! Pastors do not pastor devils and demons. They do not counsel devils and demons, they cast them out!

Don't let the devil use that whole thing of "the pastor's heart" to cause you to just accept everything that comes along:

"Well, you have got to have a pastor's heart."

"I do. That's why I'm telling you that you have to leave."

"What do you mean?"

"There is the exit sign. E-X-I-T spells exit, so exit here. Don't let the doors hit you on the way out."

> *Pastors do not pastor devils and demons. They do not counsel devils and demons, they cast them out!*

SUBSTANCE BRINGS REALITY, WHICH BRINGS RESULTS

> *The substance brings the reality, which brings the results.*

We look for the substance, we look for the reality of that which we are doing in the church, and we look for the results. The substance brings the reality, which brings the results. If there are no results, then go back to the drawing board. Ministers, go to your filing cabinet, pull out all your messages, and check the results. Throw out anything without a result. Some preachers would be shocked that they have to get rid of most of what they are preaching.

It's time for the Church to return to the *demonstration* of the power of the Holy Spirit. Somebody says, "You can't do that Sunday morning." Well, the people don't come any other time. If you can't do it Sunday morning, when can you do it? Some churches say you can't demonstrate the power of the Holy Spirit on a Sunday morning, and yet, they will spend two hours counseling a marriage that's about to break up because they wouldn't demonstrate the power of God in a Sunday morning service. They let the counseling take up their Tuesday, Wednesday, Thursday, and Friday mornings, and they run around frantically trying to do all week what the Holy Spirit would do on a Sunday morning, if they just gave Him the opportunity to do what He can do. There has to be substance, and there has to be results.

It's time for the Church to return to the demonstration of the power of the Holy Spirit.

REASONS WHY THE WIND IS LOST
So how do churches lose the Wind of God? Because it's amazing how many churches which began in great revival, are today, nothing more than mausoleums.

Firstly, it's because of complacency. "Well, we don't want to rock the boat or disrupt the status quo. Things are really good around here. We have over 10,000 members, and things are just great. We have become acceptable in the community, and it's just wonderful." But many times, the boat doesn't need rocking, it needs sinking!

Secondly, it's because of compromise. Churches and ministers want to become acceptable to those around them. They are tired of being called radicals, crazy, off the wall, and a cult.

And they are tired of being labeled extreme, and they'd like to come back into the mainstream.

Thirdly, it's because people criticize the move of God. And I can't believe that people who have really been touched by God, would get up and say what they do about the Holy Spirit, or criticize Him or the anointing! I can't believe it, but it happens.

Fourthly, it's because of the cares of this life. And finally, it's because religion and tradition come in. And when the Wind of God is lost, people find themselves in the wilderness just like the children of Israel. They are in a place in a famine.

In the last 100 years, we saw the outbreak of the Welsh revival. In 1904, a young man by the name of Evan Roberts who was 26 years old, preached and the fire of God hit Wales. One hundred and fifty thousand people were saved. That revival lasted just over a year, until a woman by the name of Jessie Penn-Lewis grabbed ahold of him and talked him right out of the move of God. And Evan Roberts went back as a recluse and left the move of God. You never heard about him after that. He could have shaken the whole of the United Kingdom if it had not been for that crazy woman. And if you get ahold of her writings, you will read how she basically attacked the whole move of God.

The outbreak of Azusa Street in 1906 lasted several years, but stopped because they allowed everything. They let anybody get up and do whatever they wanted to do. You can't do that. You can't do that under the guise of freedom. Somebody's got to be in charge of the meeting. Someone's got to say, "Yes," and "No," and it must be somebody who knows the ways of the Wind. Now if you have somebody running the meeting who doesn't know the ways of the Wind, he'd look like a Canadian goose lost in the thunderstorm. That's why, the real importance is placed upon the leader of the meeting really getting to know the ways of the Wind of the Spirit. Because if you don't know, you'll start allowing things that are not God. And when you allow things to happen that are not God, the people sitting there begin to feel uneasy. Then when the leadership says nothing about it, they just leave it. So you need to correct it. I've said in meetings, "Stop that right now!" Other people were still being touched by the move of God, and then this individual quit doing what they were doing, and everybody felt safe. Because they said, "If somebody gets out of line, Pastor will stop them."

PROTECT THE ANOINTING

You have got to be totally bold in the pulpit. Don't allow somebody to just walk in and start taking over your service. I had a minister's wife get mad at me and shout out in the middle of a meeting. I was trying to be nice to her but we eventually had to throw her out. She punched one of the deacons and walked up by the back wall of the church. There were some people that got upset because we threw her out. I said, "No, it's not her forum. It's not her place to come here and speak. We're not even interested in her opinion."

I would never go to a meeting and because I didn't like what was being said, stand up in the middle of it. You really have to be smoking some bad weed to do that. I would just leave quietly. I wouldn't even slam the door. I'd just disappear and you'd never see me again.

You can't just have everybody do everything they want to do. In the Welsh revival, it was a woman who stopped the revival. In the Azusa Street revival, it was just the leadership that allowed everything to happen that stopped the revival.

I believe we need to have meetings where we allow people

to come and minister, but you have to be very careful. If you allow somebody to come, you'd better know who they are. You don't allow just anybody to come walking out and lay hands on people. You don't know where those hands have been.

Someone says, "You are trying to control the revival." No, I'm *protecting* the revival. I have warned several of the places that have had great revivals. I've said, "If you don't quit doing what you're doing, you won't have it anymore." And today, they don't have it anymore because they never listened. They thought I was trying to control the move of God. I was not trying to control it, I was trying to protect it. You *must* protect the anointing.

4

THE NECESSITY OF THE ANOINTING:

PART TWO

It's All About Yieldedness

I mentioned in the previous chapter about protecting the anointing and not letting just anyone lay hands on people in meetings. This is so important. You have crazy people come to the meetings who say, "I'm a spiritual layer on of hands, and I travel around," but you don't know where they have come from. They could have been shacking up in a motel with whomever, and then they come to the meeting and start laying hands on people in your church! And because you don't want to offend them, you say, "Oh yeah, brother. Lay hands on them!"

RUN THE DEVILS OUT

Don't you know the devil sends people to churches on assignment? There are several people we've thrown out of The River and I've said to them, "You can't come here anymore."

"But we want to."

"Well, you're not going to."

Even an owner of a restaurant, if he had somebody always coming and sitting, and interfering with the other customers, would say, "Let me tell you right now, if you walk back onto this restaurant property, things are not going to be well with you." And it's the same way with the church.

People may say, "That's because you're not a pastor," but they can go ahead and pastor the devil, but I am not doing that. Several months before he went home to be with the Lord, Brother John Osteen said to me, "The key to pastoring is just staying put and running every devil out of town." And he didn't just mean some "thing" floating around "up there," he meant people who come into the church carrying passengers. Either they want to be free or they don't want to be free. If they don't want to be free, there's no place for them. I'll give everybody a chance, but if they don't want to be free, then their time is up and their meter has expired. I'll say, "Your time is up. I love you, but you are out of here. I'm protecting the other people." That's *true* pastoring!

Pastoring is not accommodating them, making them a home cell leader, and putting them over the Sunday school just to keep their behind in a pew. But in America, people would rather have behinds in the pew than hearts in Heaven. I want hearts in Heaven. I'll make sure that whoever God gives us here at The River is going to Heaven. *They are going to go to Heaven!* I'm not going to stand before God and have Him say to me, "You know Rodney, your ministry was so effective that 80 percent of your church split hell wide open."

Wouldn't it be terrible if you got to Heaven and you were a pastor of a 30,000-member church, and you couldn't even find more than 200 of your members because you never preached repentance or, you never talked about restitution, and you never talked about forgiveness?

IT'S NOT ABOUT BUILDING A CHURCH
Everybody just wants to build a church, and it seems it doesn't even matter how they do it. They might have ladies in bikinis taking up the offering, and they call their church "Heavenly Hooters." I'm not saying there are churches doing that, but people are using tactics to get people to come to church.

We were reading a local paper here in Tampa that goes out to every house, and Adonica came to me and said, "You won't believe this. There is a church here that is telling people they are welcome to come and not to bring their checkbook." In other words, they don't ask for money—you can leave your checkbook and wallet at home. They're not interested in blessing, they're interested in religion.

They said, "No crazy stuff happens. But the pastor is funny," which means they don't have the joy of the Lord, but the pastor is funny. That's really great! So the pastor's going to get up and tell a "Bubba" joke and everyone will laugh. That's just wonderful. People would rather have a Bubba joke than a move of God! That's like advertising, "Everybody who attends an evening service will get free lottery tickets."

In the 1920s, we saw a signs-and-wonders movement with Aimee Semple McPherson and others, like Smith Wigglesworth. In 1947, there was a healing revival. In the 1960s, it was the charismatic revival. In the 1970s, the Word-and-teaching revival. In the 1980s, it was church growth, but I don't know if you could call that a revival. It didn't really look like it. A lot of buildings went up, and most of them were empty. I had to go and preach in them and try to fill them. You don't need a big building to have a move of God. You need a big building to impress somebody, but I'm not building a building to impress another preacher! Here at The River, we are in the building process right now, but we have only embarked on this because we are following the Wind of the Spirit of God. The Wind is blowing us and directing us, and everything is paid in full!

THE END-TIME MOVE OF GOD
Let me close with this: I predict that this end-time move of God will be a combination of everything that we've seen from the Book of Acts until now. But it will be an explosion of the Spirit of God of such magnitude and such intensity. The Wind I'm talking about will be a category 5 hurricane of the Spirit of God on the Earth that will result in the greatest move of God the world has ever seen. It will bring in the greatest harvest of souls. And I predict it to be a quick work. It might be four or five years, and then we'll be out of here. I'm not meaning five years from now, but rather when it breaks in intensity. It'll be a quick work, and then we'll be out of here.

And there won't be time for people to go flaky. There won't be time for people to go off the rails. God will just blow and, "Boom!" The harvest will be reaped, and we'll go on out. And that's what I really feel because if it is anything like history, it's always cyclical. It's a cycle that always comes around: hot-lukewarm-cold; hot-lukewarm-cold; hot-lukewarm-cold. But we don't have time to go hot-lukewarm-cold. Hell is too hot, Heaven is too real, and the time is too short to go hot-lukewarm-cold. It's just a case of the Spirit of God touching the hearts of people, them grabbing ahold of the move of God and running with it, and reaping the harvest of souls. That's what it's about.

I predict that this end-time move of God will be a combination of everything that we've seen from the Book of Acts until now. But it will be an explosion of the Spirit of God of such magnitude and such intensity. The Wind I'm talking about will be a category 5 hurricane of the Spirit of God on the Earth that will result in the greatest move of God the world has ever seen. It will bring in the greatest harvest of souls. And I predict it to be a quick work.

IT'S ABOUT PEOPLE BEING EMPOWERED TO BE USED BY GOD
Yes, we need to build churches. Yes, we need to train people, but let me tell you about when I went to a great church in Asia. I gave a call for people who would go to evangelize Asia, and people streamed forward. There were probably 1,500 people that streamed forward weeping and crying. I called out people and said, "God has called you. You are called to go to Thailand." And I started naming all the Asian countries, and the people were standing, literally shaking under the power of God.

And the pastor got right up behind me and said to the individuals, "You are not ready. Go and sit down." In effect, I had wasted my message, it was redundant. He threw water on all those people, just like that.

And basically, do you know what he was saying? He didn't realize it, but what he was saying was, "My ministry has been a failure." The reason why he said they weren't ready was because he would have rather had them stay sitting in the pews, working a job, and bringing in the tithes, than have them rise up, go forth, and preach the Gospel.

And you might say to me, "But Pastor Rodney, what

if people aren't ready?" Well, if they go out there and they flounder, they'll come right back. If they are really a part of you, they'll be right back. They'll look at you and say, "I think we kind of just stepped out prematurely," and do you know what you'll do? You'll just smile and say, "Come on back." And they'll come right back, and then they'll go out again. The only way to step out is to step out and make mistakes and find out where you fit in. Haven't you made a bunch of mistakes? And don't you think that you will make some mistakes from now until Jesus comes back? But you have to pray that the mistakes will be fewer than you've ever made before.

TEACH PEOPLE TO YIELD AND LET THEM GO WHERE THE SPIRIT LEADS

If you don't release people, then you don't trust your ministry, and you don't trust the anointing upon your life to raise people up.

We've got to give people opportunity. If people feel called to go, I have never stopped anyone unless I really believe that God has another plan for them. And I can count the number on one hand of those to whom I have said, "No, I don't feel it's right now." The rest of them I just said, "Yes." Because we are to empower people.

And if you don't release people, then you don't trust your ministry, and you don't trust the anointing upon your life to raise people up. We have people all the time leaving from The River, planting churches, planting Bible schools, and going to the foreign fields. We've graduated thousands of students. And it's hard sometimes, because you see the people coming, you see the potential of what they have, and you would really just like to keep them because then, that is easy on you.

It is hard when people say they feel to move on, because I'd rather have kept them. But they say, "Pastor, you've been teaching on vision. You've been teaching on dreams, and you've awakened something on the inside of us. We have to go because of what you've been preaching," and then I think, *Oh, that's just great. I should have kept my mouth shut!*

If I preached a dead message, I could probably keep most people here. But if you preach what I preach about a stirring of the Holy Ghost, if you preach about yielding to the Spirit of God, if you preach about rising up and fulfilling your vision and dream, if you preach about going to the nations of the world, then what's going to happen? Signs are going to follow the preaching of the Word! People are going to rise up, and people are going to get bold. If you preach about boldness, they are going to get bold. If you preach about vision, they are going to have vision. If you preach about dreams, they are going to have dreams. If you preach about going into all the world, they are going to go into all the world. If you're preaching about believing God for big things, they'll believe God for big things.

So I'd rather suffer from the results of the message that way than from the results of the message the other way. Because when it's all said and done, I want to stand before the Lord and say, "Those people that You gave to us, we did our best to put everything into them and to launch them to go and obey the call of God." What we put in them is not something that's tradition and it is not something that's religion. It's something that has *substance*.

RAISE PEOPLE THAT HAVE SUBSTANCE
There is a young man out of our Bible school who when he first came, and was always joking around and being goofy. He went through Bible school and really didn't know which way to go. And he'd come to me with all these ideas and say, "Pastor, I'm going to do this." And I'd just say, "Chill out. Calm down. Just take it easy. Finish school before you run off anywhere." Then he came to me one day and told me he was heading to a certain place. And I looked at him and I said, "Are you sure?" And later he told me, "When you said that, I felt my heart sink. I thought to myself, *Oh no. He knows something.*" Well, he went there, and within a week, he was back. He said, "I couldn't stay. I was in the wrong place."

When he first came to The River, he was probably around twenty-two/twenty-three years old, and it is exciting to see these kids growing up and maturing in the things of God. That's what's so exciting about pastoring, seeing people grow and mature.

In the first days, they are in every prayer line and are always crying. Things are getting hard, but then they come to the place where they are praying for other people, and you see them mature and grow, taking on the characteristics of someone for whom God is working in their life. And instead of opening their mouth and changing feet, they are actually speaking life, and that's exciting. Then that means your ministry is being a success.

He got married, and they went over to South Africa to visit his in-laws. While he was there, his mother-in-law started inviting people to the house, and he prayed for them. All these people came to the house to see this Bible school student for prayer, and they got healed. Then somebody heard he was from The River and they said, "Would you come and hold a

THE NECESSITY OF THE ANOINTING: PART TWO

meeting?" So he did, and when he got there he told me, "Pastor, the moment I walked in the door, I knew there was a poverty devil there." So he looked at the people and said, "The reason why you are in this mess is because you people don't give." And then he laid into them and hit them up one side and down the other. He said, "I didn't come here to get invited back." Of course, I don't know where he got some of this terminology and this boldness from! But he said, "You've got a poverty devil, and some of you need an enema." He used everything I teach and just threw it all into one message.

But you know, God gave him a mighty breakthrough. There were other seasoned ministers who went to South Africa and struggled, but in one week, this young man and his wife were so blessed financially. The power of God hit the place, and he got invited here, there, and everywhere. He was just radical.

Then he called me up because they were planning to go out to Hawaii to help a church over there. He said to me, "We're heading for Hawaii." I said, "Why?" He said, "To go and help." I said, "That's not what God wants you to do." "What are you talking about, Pastor?" he asked. I said, "Don't you understand the Lord has launched your ministry? Don't you understand that you are actually going to step out of the ministry by going to help another ministry? Because when you were just seeing your in-laws, God actually launched your ministry."

And then it was like a light went on. And the Lord said to me, "If he'll go back, I want you to pay his air tickets back." I didn't know at that moment he was sitting at his computer with emails coming of the miracles and healings in the services he had taken, and he was there crying as he remembered the move of God. And that day he said, "Lord, if Pastor will call me and say, 'I'll pay your air tickets,' I'll use that as a sign that

You want me to go back to southern Africa." And that morning, I asked someone to get hold of him and tell him to come and see me. He walked in my office and I said, "The Lord spoke to me to tell you if you will go back to South Africa, I'll pay your air tickets." He looked at me and burst out crying.

And I had the privilege of sticking him and his wife on an airplane. They gave away their cars; they radically grabbed ahold of the giving teaching. And he went with a brand-new laptop, and everything brand-new. He said, "Pastor, I have more money than I know what to do with. Finances are coming in from everywhere." Some people can't even raise support, but here was this young man with money coming in from every side. He got on the plane and went back to South Africa. Later, I got an email telling me that he went into a high school and 800 kids got saved.

In his meetings, people ran and threw offerings on the platform, jewelry, watches, and all kind of stuff. So I don't even have to worry about whether he's going to make it or not. I know he's going to make it. You know why? Because he doesn't have tradition, and he doesn't have religion. He's got substance.

We have got to put substance into our people. We're going to make sure our people get it. Now some won't get it, so you have to grab them and shake them until their false teeth rattle and until they do get it. You have almost got to get in their faces. The ones who have a pure heart will grab it. I tell people all the time, you can find a lot of nice religious churches around, please use them. Don't use us.

There's a purpose for The River, and we know what our purpose is. I'm not here to build a religious institution. I'll walk away from everything here in a heartbeat because I will not sacrifice the "nation of Egypt" on an altar of religion and tradition.

If you think I'm attached to The River property and to whatever's going on around The River, you are totally mistaken. I will not sacrifice what God is doing in "Egypt"—that is, what God is doing in some of the nations of the world, for religion and tradition. That's the bottom line. That's why we have all-night prayer meetings. Not everyone can stay all night, but people come for a few hours. Not everybody can pray all night and that's fine, but they are going to pray for some time. I'm not going to stand before God and He say, "You never taught my people to pray." You have to have substance.

DON'T LET RELIGION AND TRADITION RESTRICT YOU

You must follow the Wind of the Spirit of God. I feel so sorry for pastors who are stuck in a church that is run by a board. The pastors have to report to the board who tell them what to preach, and what they can do and can't do. Basically, they just stop the Wind in their church. They stop the Wind!

Whenever we've gone to have revival in the local church and the pastor said to me, "You can't do this. You can't do that," I've looked at him and said, "You don't really want me, do you?"

"No. No, I want you."

"No, you want yourself. Because you say that I can't do this, and I can't do that, and you *know* that's what I do. So if I can't do this and can't do that, and can't do the other thing, then I can't do anything. And then I can't be me. You are stopping the Wind, so there'll be no Wind. So just have yourself a merry little Christmas. If you want me to come to preach, you have to turn me loose." Someone says, "What's going to happen if you are turned loose?" I don't know. We might have several things. We might have a revival. We might have a riot. It's whatever it takes. Don't let people put restraints on you. They'll try to.

They'll try to clip your wings, but don't let them do it.

As I said earlier, when we did the Australian tour, the people came out by the tens of thousands, but we had a lot of "looky-loos." But it was not a state fair and it was not a circus. There's a price to pay. No matter how great the joy is, there is a deep seriousness to everything that goes on. People misinterpreted the joy and thought it was a joke. But it's *not* a joke.

If you come to a meeting expecting nothing, you will get it. I went to a church where the people were told to go and lie down. I walked around and said, "Stand up. What are you doing?" And they said, "Well, people laid their hands on us before and nothing happened. So, they just told to us to lie down." I thought, *Talk about tradition, this is revival tradition*! *They are all lying down. They can lie down on their bed at home, but not here*!

I said to the pastor, "What are you doing?" He said, "Well, it might help them to break through." I said, "What a bunch of garbage. Who taught you that?" The amount of ignorance has gone to seed. It defies description. I've never seen anything like it in my life.

DON'T LET FEAR HOLD YOU BACK

> *Don't allow tradition to dictate to you what you think you have to do at the moment. Follow the Spirit of God, because that's where the life will be.*

Don't let religion and tradition restrict you, but also, don't let fear hold you back. I have a friend who was a drug dealer. He was in prison, and an angel walked into the cell. Now, he has one of the greatest churches in New York City. What do you do when the angel walks into your cell? You become a pastor in the Bronx, and to become a pastor in the Bronx, you need to have an angel walk into your cell!

Maybe you are reading this and you are a little afraid to really get out there, because you know that you'd be the life of the party. You're just a little afraid to really yield because you know that if you would, you'd smoke the house. If you really just yielded yourself to the Spirit of God when the anointing comes on you, you'd be like nothing else we've ever seen in recent history. But don't let fear hold you back.

You must follow the Wind. There will be times you'll get in the pulpit and the Lord will tell you not to preach the message you've prepared. You might be a singer, and you'll have a scheduled song, and the Lord will say, "Don't sing that song." Just follow the Wind of the Spirit of God. I don't care if it's a special Mother's Day message. If the Lord says, "Forget it," then forget it. Even if you have to wait another year to preach that message. Because God probably has something better for the mothers.

Don't allow tradition to dictate to you what you think you have to do at the moment. Follow the Spirit of God, because that's where the life will be. When you follow the Spirit of God, that's where the life will be.

DON'T LET OFFENSE BE A BLOCKAGE

Finally, never let offense, bitterness, or unforgiveness come and block the Wind of God. I've had singers come to my meetings, and they have gotten offended because they didn't get to sing. I said to them, "You'll get to sing when I feel the Wind of God for that, but until then, just sit and jump in the river of God like everybody else. I'm sorry, but I can't accommodate you just because you 'have voice, will travel.' There's more that's at stake here than just you singing."

God sends us some of the best singers in the world. And sometimes, we'll have five of them all sitting down and lined up like planes on the runway. They know that they may sing or they may not sing. If they sing, wonderful, if they don't, wonderful.

If somebody gets all bent out of shape because they were scheduled, they have the wrong spirit anyway. You might have scheduled a meeting in your church with a guest evangelist, but God moves in a different way. Pay him not to preach, and just give him an offering. Say, "I'll give you an offering, pay your hotel, and you can have a vacation. I'll pay you just like it was going to be in revival. I'll pay you to shut up. I'll bless you."

EXPERIENCE THE FREEDOM OF FOLLOWING THE WIND

The Wind is blowing, and we have so little time before the return of the King. We stand on the brink of the greatest revival and the greatest harvest of souls that the world has ever seen. You have been handpicked by God to live in this hour.

You are not those who will live the mundane. You are not those whose life will go into oblivion, whose life will go into eternity with nothing to carry. You are those handpicked by the Master who will carry this Good News, the Gospel, with power, signs, and mighty wonders, seeing the nations of the Earth shaken. But will you let Him use you? Will you let go of religion and tradition? Will you let go of fear?

The Wind bloweth where it listeth. The Wind is blowing and no man can stop it. You can *choose* to follow the Wind. You can *choose* to let the Wind of God blow *in* you and *through* you. If you do, your life will never be the same. The decision is yours. All you have to do is just throw up your hands and say, "Lord, I don't feel within myself that I even have what it takes, but God, I just yield myself to You. Wherever You want to blow, wherever You want me to go, I'll go, I'll do what You want me to do, I'll say what You want me to say, and I'll be what You want me to be. I will follow the ways of Your Wind."

POSTSCRIPT

If you have been blessed and challenged by this book, please write to us here at our Tampa office or email us at testimonies@revival.com

  We would love to hear from you. If you were stirred up and challenged to change and allow God to do His work in you, we pray that God would use you in a wonderful way to touch a lost and dying world.

Write to:
Revival Ministries International
P.O. Box 292888 Tampa, FL 33687

You can also reach us at www.revival.com/prayer/testimony
or
call 1(813) 971-9999

For souls and another Great Spiritual Awakening in America,
                              –DR. RODNEY HOWARD-BROWNE

ABOUT THE AUTHOR

Drs. Rodney and Adonica Howard-Browne are the founders of Revival Ministries International, The River at Tampa Bay Church, and River University in Tampa, Florida.

In December of 1987, Rodney, along with his wife, Adonica, and their three children, Kirsten, Kelly, and Kenneth, moved from their native land, South Africa, to the United States called by God as missionaries from Africa to America. The Lord had spoken through Rodney in a word of prophecy and declared, "As America has sown missionaries over the last two hundred years, I am going to raise up people from other nations to come to the United States of America. I am sending a mighty revival to America."

In April of 1989, the Lord sent a revival of signs and wonders and miracles that began in a church in Clifton Park, New York, that has continued until today, resulting in thousands of people being touched and changed as they encounter the presence of the living God. God is still moving today—saving, healing, delivering, restoring, and setting free!

Drs. Rodney and Adonica's second daughter, Kelly, was born with an incurable lung disease called cystic fibrosis. This demonic disease slowly destroyed her lungs. Early on Christmas morning 2002, at the age of eighteen, she ran out of lung capacity and

ABOUT THE AUTHOR

breathed out her last breath. They placed her into the arms of her Lord and Savior and then vowed a vow. First, they vowed that the devil would pay for what he had done to their family. Secondly, they vowed to do everything in their power, with the help of the Lord, to win one hundred million souls to Jesus and to put $1 billion into world missions and the harvest of souls.

When Drs. Rodney and Adonica became naturalized citizens of the United States of America, in 2008 and 2004 respectively, they took the United States Oath of Allegiance, which declares, "I will support and defend the Constitution and laws of the United States of America against all enemies, foreign and domestic." They took this oath to heart. They love America, are praying for this country, and are trusting God to see another Great Awakening sweep across this land.

Believing for this Great Spiritual Awakening, Drs. Rodney and Adonica conducted Celebrate America D.C., a soul winning event. They preached the Gospel of Jesus Christ for fifty nights in Washington, D.C., and surrounding areas from 2014 to 2019. Through the evangelism efforts on the streets, in the halls of Congress, and the nightly altar calls, 58,033 individuals made decisions for Jesus Christ.

During Celebrate America, in July of 2014, at the Daughters of the American Revolution Constitution Hall, Dr. Rodney executed a restraining order against the structure that is holding America in captivity, binding it and rendering it powerless and ineffective, from the Supreme Court, to the White House, to the Executive Branch, Congress, and the Senate, in the Name of Jesus. He commanded the Church in America to wake up and for the people of God to come out of their slumber. He declared that it is time to take the land.

During the Covid era, Drs. Rodney and Adonica took a

ABOUT THE AUTHOR

stand for the Gospel of Jesus Christ. As a result, Dr. Rodney was wrongfully arrested at his home on March 30, 2020, for holding a church service at The River at Tampa Bay Church on Sunday, March 29.

As a result of his arrest, Florida Governor Ron DeSantis declared attendance at churches, synagogues, and houses of worship to be an essential activity. Dr. Rodney's arrest freed up every church in Florida to meet. All the charges were dropped by the Thirteenth Judicial Circuit State Attorney on May 15, 2020, and the date of his arrest and criminal record were expunged by Circuit Court Judge John N. Conrad on February 22, 2021.

Drs. Rodney and Adonica continue to take a stand for the Word of God and for billions around the world whose right to worship freely was removed and has not been, or perhaps will never be, restored. The Stand nightly services have continued for over 1,300 nights, as they stand for their brothers and sisters around the world who cannot stand freely.

With a passion for souls and a passion to revive and mobilize the Body of Christ, Drs. Rodney and Adonica have conducted revivals and soul winning efforts throughout ninety-two nations with the 300 City Tour, Good News campaigns, R.M.I. Revivals, the Great Awakening Tours, and The Stand. As a result, over 46,407,883 precious people have come to Christ, and tens of thousands of believers have been revived and mobilized to preach the Gospel of Jesus Christ. For more information, visit revival.com.

CONNECT

Please visit revival.com or rodneyhowardbrowne.com for our latest updates and news. Many of our services are live online. Additionally, many of our recorded services are available on Video on Demand.

For a listing of Drs. Rodney and Adonica Howard-Browne's products and itinerary, please visit revival.com. To download the soul-winning tools for free, please visit revival.com and click on Soul-winning Tools.

- **Like us on Facebook:**
  Facebook.com/rodneyadonicahowardbrowne
- **Follow us on Twitter:**
  @rhowardbrowne
- **Follow us on YouTube:**
  YouTube.com/rodneyhowardbrowne
- **Follow us on Instagram:**
  @rodneyhowardbrowne
- **Follow us on Rumble:**
  @rhowardbrowne

OTHER BOOKS AND RESOURCES BY RODNEY HOWARD-BROWNE

BOOKS

Communion: The Table of the Lord
The Call of God
Kingdom Business
Leadership Principles
The Phantom Virus
Socialism Under the Microscope
God's Top Ten
Perpetual Harvest
Killing the Planet: How a Financial Cartel Doomed Mankind
The Anointing
The Killing of Uncle of Sam: The Demise of the United States of America
Thoughts on Stewardship
The Coming Revival
The Touch of God
The Gifts of the Holy Spirit
The Reality of Life After Death
Seeing Jesus as He Really Is
The Curse Is Not Greater than the Blessing
How to Increase and Release the Anointing
School of the Spirit
The Anointing
Manifesting the Holy Ghost
What Gifts Do You Bring the King?
Prayer Journal
Sowing in Famine

OTHER BOOKS AND RESOURCES

AUDIO CDS
Prayer Time
Weapons of Our Warfare
Becoming One Flesh
Faith
Flowing in the Holy Ghost
How to Flow in the Anointing
Igniting the Fire
In Search of the Anointing
Prayer that Moves Mountains
Accelerate
The Camels are Coming
Pray Without Ceasing Vol.1
Pray Without Ceasing Vol.2
The Touch of God
Mountain Moving Prayer
Having an Encounter with God
God's Mandate
The Anointing is Transferable
Dealing with Offenses
The Vow and the Decree
Whosoever Can Get Whatsoever
Run to the Water
Demonstrations of the Spirit
   and of Power
The Double Portion
More Than Laughter
The Hand of the Lord

Running the Heavenly Race
The Holy Spirit, His
   Purpose & Power
The Power to Create Wealth

Walking in Heaven's Light
All These Blessings
A Surplus of Prosperity
The Joy of the Lord is
   My Strength
Prayer Secrets
Communion–The Table
   of the Lord
My Roadmap
My Mission–My Purpose
My Heart
My Family
My Worship
Decreeing Faith
Ingredients of Revival
Fear Not
Matters of the Heart by Dr.
   Adonica Howard-Browne
My Treasure
My Absolutes
My Father
My Crowns
My Comforter & Helper
Renewing the Mind
Seated in High Places
Triumphant Entry
Merchandising and Trafficking
   the Anointing
My Prayer Life
My Jesus
Seeing Jesus as He Really Is
Exposing the World's System

OTHER BOOKS AND RESOURCES

Living in the Land of
 Visions & Dreams
Kingdom Business
Taking Cities in the
 Land of Giants
Spiritual Hunger
The Two Streams

MP3 CDS

The Phantom Virus
Socialism Under the Microscope
Killing the Planet: How
 a Financial Cartel
 Doomed Mankind
The Killing of Uncle Sam
The Touch of God:
 The Anointing
Knowing the Person of the
 Holy Spirit
The Love Walk
How to Hear the Voice of God
Matters of the Heart
Exposing the World's System
How to Be Led by the Holy Spirit
The Anointing
The Ways of the Wind

DVDS

Mountain Moving Prayer
How to Personally Lead
 Someone to Jesus
The Fire of God
Vision for America
Living the Christian Lifestyle

No Limits No Boundaries
The Curse is Not Greater Than
 the Blessing
God's Glory Manifested through
 Special Anointings
Good News New York
Jerusalem Ablaze
The Mercy of God by Dr.
 Adonica Howard-Browne
Are You a Performer or
 a Minister?
Revival at ORU
 Volume 1, 2 & 3
The Realms of God
Singapore Ablaze
The Coat My Father Gave Me
Have You Ever Wondered What
 Jesus Was Like?
There Is a Storm Coming
 (Recorded live from
 Good News New York)
Budapest, Hungary Ablaze
The Camels Are Coming
Power Evangelism
Taking Cities in the
 Land of Giants
Renewing the Mind
Triumphant Entry
Merchandising and Trafficking
 the Anointing
Doing Business with God
Accelerate

OTHER BOOKS AND RESOURCES

MUSIC
The Stand 2023
Youth Fire Week EP
Kids Fire Week EP
Nothing Is Impossible
By His Stripes
Run with Fire
The Sweet Presence of Jesus
Eternity with Kelly
    Howard-Browne
Live from The River
You're Such a Good God to Me
Howard-Browne
    Family Christmas
He Lives
Anointed—The Decade
    of the '80s
Live Summer Campmeeting '15
Live Summer Campmeeting '16
Haitian Praise
No Limits
Christmas Extravaganza At The
    River Vol. 1 & 2

THE RIVER AT TAMPA BAY CHURCH

The River at Tampa Bay Church was founded on December 1, 1996. At the close of 1996, the Lord planted within Pastors Rodney and Adonica's heart the vision and desire to start a church in Tampa. With a heart for the lost and to minister to those who had been touched by revival, they implemented that vision and began The River at Tampa Bay, with the motto, "Church with a Difference."

Over 575 people joined them for the first Sunday morning service on December 1, 1996. Over the years, the membership has grown and the facilities have changed, yet these three things have remained constant since the church's inception ... dynamic praise and worship, anointed preaching and teaching of the Word, and powerful demonstrations of the Holy Spirit and power. The Lord spoke to Pastor Rodney's heart to feed the people, touch the people, and love the people. With this in mind and heart, the goal of The River is:

To become a model revival church where people from all over the world can come and be touched by God. Once they have been not only touched, but changed, they are ready to be launched out into the harvest field with the anointing of God.

To have a church that is multi-racial, representing a cross

section of society from rich to poor from all nations, bringing people to a place of maturity in their Christian walk.

To see the lost, the backslidden and the unsure come to a full assurance of their salvation.

To be a home base for Revival Ministries International and all of its arms. A base offering strength and support to the vision of R.M.I. to see America shaken with the fires of revival, then to take that fire to the far-flung corners of the globe.

To break the mold of religious tradition and thinking.

To be totally dependent upon the Holy Spirit for His leading and guidance as we lead others deeper into the River of God.

Our motto: Church with a Difference.

For The River at Tampa Bay's service times and directions, please, visit revival.com or call (813) 971-9999. Location: The River at Tampa Bay Church, 3738 River International Dr., Tampa, FL 33610.

RIVER UNIVERSITY

River University is a place where men and women of all ages, backgrounds, and experiences can gather together to study and experience the glory of God. River University is not a traditional Bible school. It is a Holy Ghost training center, birthed specifically for those whose strongest desire is to know Christ and to make Him known.

The vision for River University is plain: To train men and women in the spirit of revival for ministry in the 21st century. The school was birthed in 1997, with a desire to train up revivalists for the 21st century. It is a place where the Word of God and the Holy Spirit come together to produce life, birth ministries, and launch them out. River University is a place where ministries are sent to the far-flung corners of the globe to spread revival, and to bring in a harvest of souls for the Kingdom of God.

While preaching in many nations and regions of the world, Dr. Rodney Howard-Browne has observed that all the people of the earth have one thing in common: a desperate need for the genuine touch of God. From the interior of Alaska through the bush country of Africa, to the outback villages of Australia, to the cities of North America, people are tired of religion and ritualistic worship. They are crying out for the reality of His presence. River University is dedicated to training believers how to live, minister, and flow in the anointing.

The Word will challenge those attending to find clarity in their calling, and be changed by the awesome presence of God. This is the hour of God's power, not just for the full-time minister, but for all of God's people who are hungry for more. Whether you are a housewife or an aspiring evangelist, River University will deepen your relationship and experience in the Lord, and provide you with a new perspective on how to reach others with God's life-changing power.

Programs Include:

- River Bible Institute

- River School of Worship

- River School of Government

- River Bible Español

You can be saturated in the Word and the Spirit of God at River University. Since 1997, River University has graduated over 10,159 students (including our subsidiary schools). River University is the place where you will be empowered to reach your high calling and set your world on fire with revival. For more information about River University, please visit revival.com, or call (813) 899-0085 or (813) 971-9999.

RIVER SCHOOL OF THE BIBLE ONLINE

River School of the Bible is our online school to train up revivalists for the 21st century. It was started so that those who are unable to come to the school in Tampa, can receive this training and impartation, anyplace worldwide. It is not a traditional Bible school. It is a Holy Ghost training center, birthed specifically for those whose strongest desire is to know Christ and to make Him known.

This program provides quality, Spirit-filled Biblical instruction, academic training, and practical education to men and women called into the five-fold ministry, or for those who desire to become better equipped in other areas of Christian service. Since 2018, over 100 students have graduated from the school. So, don't wait! God wants to raise you up to do great things for Him.

For more information, please visit revival.com/rsb, or email rsb@revival.com

GOD WANTS TO USE YOU TO BRING IN THE HARVEST OF SOULS!

The Great Commission, "Go ye into all the world and preach the Gospel to every creature," is for every believer to take personally. Every believer is to be an announcer of the Good News Gospel. When the Gospel is preached, people have an encounter with Jesus. Jesus is the only One Who can change the heart of a man, woman, child, and nation!

On the next page is a tool to assist you in sharing the Gospel with others. It is called, "The Gospel Soul-Winning Script." Please make copies of it, fold it in the center lengthwise, and read it to people. As you read it to others, you will see many come to Christ, because as stated in Romans 1:16, *"For I am not ashamed of the gospel of Christ: for it is the power of God unto salvation to every one that believeth ..."*

Please visit revival.com, click on Soul-Winning Tools, and review the many tools and videos that are freely available to help you bring in the harvest of souls. It is harvest time!

THE GOSPEL SOUL-WINNING — SCRIPT —

Has anyone ever told you that God loves you and that He has a wonderful plan for your life? I have a real quick, but important question to ask you. If you were to die this very second, do you know for sure, beyond a shadow of a doubt, that you would go to Heaven? [If "Yes"— Great, why would you say "Yes"? (If they respond with anything but "I have Jesus in my heart" or something similar to that, PROCEED WITH SCRIPT) or "No" or "I hope so" PROCEED WITH SCRIPT.]

Let me quickly share with you what the Holy Bible reads. It reads "for all have sinned and come short of the glory of God" and "for the wages of sin is death, but the gift of God is eternal life through Jesus Christ our Lord". The Bible also reads, "For whosoever shall call upon the name of the Lord shall be saved". And you're a "whosoever" right? Of course you are; all of us are.

continued on reverse side —

I'm going to say a quick prayer for you. Lord, bless (FILL IN NAME) and his/her family with long and healthy lives. Jesus, make Yourself real to him/her and do a quick work in his/her heart. If (FILL IN NAME) has not received Jesus Christ as his/her Lord and Savior, I pray he/she will do so now.

(FILL IN NAME), if you would like to receive the gift that God has for you today, say this after me with your heart and lips out loud. Dear Lord Jesus, come into my heart. Forgive me of my sin. Wash me and cleanse me. Set me free. Jesus, thank You that You died for me. I believe that You are risen from the dead and that You're coming back again for me. Fill me with the Holy Spirit. Give me a passion for the lost, a hunger for the things of God and a holy boldness to preach the gospel of Jesus Christ. I'm saved; I'm born again, I'm forgiven and I'm on my way to Heaven because I have Jesus in my heart.

As a minister of the gospel of Jesus Christ, I tell you today that all of your sins are forgiven. Always remember to run to God and not from God because He loves you and has a great plan for your life.

[Invite them to your church and get follow up info: name, address, & phone number.]

Revival Ministries International
P.O. Box 292888 • Tampa, FL 33687
(813) 971-9999 • www.revival.com

THE RIVER AT TAMPA BAY CHURCH
ALTAR CALL

CELEBRATE AMERICA
WASHINGTON, D.C.
57,498 SALVATIONS

THE STAND | 1,300 NIGHTS AND COUNTING

**THE GREAT AWAKENING BROADCAST WITH
CHRISTIAN TELEVISION NETWORK
OVER 41 MILLION RECORDED DECISIONS FOR CHRIST**

GOOD NEWS NEW YORK - 1999
MADISON SQUARE GARDEN
48,459 SALVATIONS

GOOD NEWS NEW YORK - 1999
MADISON SQUARE GARDEN
48,459 SALVATIONS

GOOD NEW SOWETO - 2004
SOWETO, SOUTH AFRICA
177,600 SALVATIONS

GOOD NEWS UMLAZI - 2005
UMLAZI, SOUTH AFRICA
286,750 SALVATIONS

SINGAPORE - 1995

THE EARLY YEARS
RODNEY, ADONICA, KIRSTEN, KELLY, & KENNETH

THE EARLY YEARS
RODNEY & ADONICA